Mind Easing

The Three-Layered Healing Plan for Anxiety and Depression

BICK WANCK, MD

Health Communications, Inc.
Deerfield Beach, Florida

www.hcibooks.com

**Library of Congress Cataloging-in-Publication Data
is available through the Library of Congress**

© 2019 Bick Wanck, MD

ISBN-13: 978-07573-2154-2 (Paperback)
ISBN-10: 07573-2154-2 (Paperback)
ISBN-13: 978-07573-2155-9 (ePub)
ISBN-10: 07573-2155-0 (ePub)

Publisher: Health Communications, Inc.
     3201 S.W. 15th Street
     Deerfield Beach, FL 33442–8190

Mind Easing is a self-help guide of suggested wellness and treatment approaches designed to assist the way your mind naturally heals from anxiety and depression. It does not take the place of wellness and treatment recommendations by trained professionals. Be sure to consult with your prescriber, therapist, or wellness professional before you try any of the suggestions in this book. It is especially important to consult with a professional before incorporating any of the suggestions in this book if you have a medical condition or a genetic predisposition to one, or if you are or think you might be pregnant. Be sure to review your healing plan with professionals before you put it into action.

All efforts have been made to ensure the accuracy of the information contained in this book as of the date of publication. The author and the publisher expressly disclaim responsibility for any adverse effects arising from the use or application of the information contained herein.

The author has no financial relationship with any manufacturer of a pharmaceutical, herbal remedy, or dietary plan or supplement, nor with any competitor of a pharmaceutical, herbal remedy, or dietary plan or supplement mentioned in this book.

The characters, events, and places portrayed in this book are fictional. Any similarities to actual people, events, or places are entirely coincidental.

Cover design by Larissa Hise Henoch
Interior design and formatting by Lawna Patterson Oldfield
Author photo by Tom Stock of Stock Studios Photography

To Romcha

Contents

Layer Three: Restoration

Introduction

The human mind is remarkable. It can actually heal itself. But there's a hitch. Sometimes healing needs our support and guidance to do it right.

That's what *Mind Easing* is all about. In this book, I show you how to construct a healing plan for your mind. Unlike a treatment plan, a healing plan works directly with your natural healing process to enhance, guide, and restore your natural flow of healing to help resolve your distress and find your way to greater ease.

I'm not suggesting that you throw away whatever you may be doing for yourself now. What I do propose is that you place it into a well-constructed healing plan. Whatever you are doing now to help your mind will likely be made safer and more effective if you do it from the new perspective I share with you.

My intention is to help you tune into your healing process and strengthen it. I show you how to work with your natural flow of healing instead of imposing hastily chosen treatments. You'll learn to make decisions about wellness, therapy, and medicine based on what would work best for your own unique style of healing.

It makes sense to work with your individual healing nature rather than ignoring or working against it, which can happen when treatment decisions don't take healing into consideration.

Together, we'll create a plan that will help you—not just now, but for the rest of your life.

The path that led me to share this healing plan with you has not always been easy. My journey has been arduous, but it has resulted in recovery, wellness, and growth. After years of violent and otherwise challenging circumstances growing up outside a small town in Appalachia and then living in an impoverished and crime-ridden inner-city neighborhood, I learned the values of perseverance, persistence, and determination. By necessity, I sought healing for myself. My mission became helping others do the same. I know what it's like to suffer, and I know what it's like to get well and flourish. I learned about the essential nature and process of healing and promoting healing the hard way. My calling and passion are to help others find their own way to wellness.

My desire to help led me to become a doctor and then a board-certified psychiatrist. During the course of my career, I became one of the founders of the American Academy of Addiction Psychiatry, taught psychiatry in several medical schools, wrote numerous scholarly articles, and gave hundreds of talks around the country.

It was, however, by successfully helping thousands over the course of three decades that I've developed the Three-Layered Healing Plan I am sharing with you. Here are some of the objectives people have met by using this approach:

- Reducing or eliminating panic and unmanageable anxiety

- Finding relief from depression and unreasonable sadness
- Managing mood swings more effectively
- Reducing and managing compulsive and addictive urges
- Establishing a healthy diet and keeping weight in a reasonable range
- Having a satisfying sex life based on love and natural urge rather than guilt, compulsion, or fear-based need
- Enjoying love and friendship unfettered by guilt, fear, and drama
- Managing and resolving the effects of childhood or adulthood trauma
- Learning the coping skills needed to deal with life's threats and disappointments
- Having faith and confidence in the capacity to heal
- Gaining wisdom from life's lessons

Mind Easing gives you a fresh perspective for meeting your challenges head-on. By approaching your goals from the stance of healing, your journey to a new way of managing your distress is more likely to be safe, sensible, and productive.

As you construct your healing plan, I recommend that you share it with those who have already earned your trust. Most therapists, bodyworkers, spiritual guides, and prescribers are healers by intention. Most will take an interest in your healing plan and encourage you to use it. Be patient with them if they are not as receptive as you would like. As long as you are clear about your healing needs, you can teach others how to help you.

This is your healing plan to share with others as you wish. The professionals you may hire to help are likely to have some useful suggestions you may wish to incorporate. As you hear their suggestions, listen to your inner voice. Do their suggestions make sense to you? Do they feel right? *Mind Easing* will help you become more aware of your natural healing process and help you decide what will best assist it.

The Three-Layered Healing Plan

Central to *Mind Easing* is the Three-Layered Healing Plan. It is a plan that assembles conventional wellness and treatment approaches in an innovative format designed to assist the natural healing process.

Layer One: Enhancement

Begin by practicing positive attitudes and healthy behaviors. *Mind Easing* presents the ABCs of healing enhancement: attitudes, behaviors, and compassionate love. In the behaviors section, you will learn how to use Mindfulness, Exercise, Diet, and Stress management (MEDS) to empower your healing.

You will find out why the enhancement of healing is something you should do even when you are not in distress. When you enhance your healing, you help your body as well as your mind. By making healing enhancements part of your daily routine, you will live longer and be in better health. You will be able to enjoy the benefits of your healing plan! Many of my patients say that healing enhancements are the best MEDS they have ever taken.

Layer Two: Guidance

You will learn about three types of guidance: conscious guidance, body and energy work, and spiritual guidance. Some people use one form of guidance while others combine two or all three. We'll work on understanding which approach will be most likely to help you.

Conscious guidance helps correct misperceptions and unhealthy responses. By using conscious guidance, psychotherapists, counselors, and life coaches can help point your healing in the right direction.

Guidance through body and energy work often requires less effort. Sometimes it can give quick relief as well as a long-term effect. Sometimes it can open your mind to what you didn't know was wrong. (Sometimes the body remembers what the mind forgets.)

Healing is, at its core, a spiritual process. It operates in wondrous ways beyond our comprehension. Surrender, faith, and spiritual opening, when properly guided, can accomplish what other forms of guidance cannot. *Mind Easing* will help you achieve a state of mind that will invite a state of grace.

Layer Three: Restoration

Sometimes you may need to get healing back on track after it's been blocked or derailed by symptoms too severe for guidance to manage alone. Restoration involves the use of medicine to reduce the intensity of symptoms like panic or despair that could otherwise overwhelm your capacity to heal. Medicine can be a lifesaver and a lifestyle saver when used correctly.

Medicine can also cause serious or even dangerous effects that can harm or block the healing process. Sometimes it is more important to stop a medicine than it is to start one. When placed within the context of healing, this question is easier to answer: Will I heal more safely and effectively with medicine, or will medicine block or impede my capacity to heal? In the pages that follow, I show you how to answer that question and then what to do next.

The Three-Layered Healing Plan has been designed to meet your unique needs by suggesting various approaches and why you may wish to choose them. It also shows you how to sequentially add layers as you need them. The Three-Layered Healing Plan provides what you need when you need it. The goal is to get you to a better place by the route you are best able to travel.

As you are discovering how to help your own mind to heal, you will be introduced to Lisa and her friends. They are fictionalized composite characters based on real people, real struggles, and real solutions. You will find through them that you are not alone in your quest for wellness. By walking with Lisa and her friends as they find their way to greater ease and comfort, you will better understand how the Three-Layered Healing Plan can work for you.

My Healing Rebellion

I have been a practicing psychiatrist for more than thirty years, but I am not your typical shrink. I have been on a healing rebellion for many years. When I first started medical school, I thought I would learn how to help people heal. Instead, I was taught how to treat illness. Although treating illness is a necessary part of helping people heal, I felt that focusing only on treatment missed the big picture. It made no sense to me to give so little attention to the miracle of healing. It seemed like Western medicine missed the most important point.

My frustration about the lack of emphasis on healing in medicine nearly drove me away entirely. After I graduated from medical school,

I wanted to hide the degree. The last thing I wanted was for someone to call me "doctor." With its lack of emphasis on healing, I resisted my association with the medical system.

I decided to give myself a year to think this all over. I lived out of a van, built custom furniture, meditated, and wrote. When I ran out of money, I picked up lifeguarding jobs and taught children to swim. I traveled to Peru, where I climbed mountains and explored the jungle.

While in the jungle, I found my way to an isolated tribe and met a shaman. The shaman did not trust me. I had the wrong look, smell, and attitude. I was required to join a ceremonial circle and drink a green, frothy liquid from a carved wooden bowl. I was closely observed as I started hallucinating colorful fish leaping out of the ground. I passed the test and was received warmly.

The shaman taught me how to sense when it was safe to swim in the river—when the piranha would not attack. He taught me that all things are united and that energy flows through it all. He showed me how he could direct the flow of energy to result in healing. His ability to transcend ordinary reality and bring healing energy to a sufferer was fascinating and amazingly effective.

Though his skill was way beyond my ability, he taught me to pay better attention to suffering and to realize that healing could be strengthened in unexpected ways.

The shaman's lessons complemented stories I was taught as a child, like the Seneca (Native American) creation myth along with stories of spirit healing. I had been taught early on to honor the connection between all things and to understand that all is unified by a great power. As a young man, I spent time in longhouses, corn festivals, and sweat lodges. I accepted the fact that the fundamental process of healing was not well understood or described by Western medicine. I knew that my calling was to serve the greater power of healing. I just didn't know how to get there.

When I first went into the jungle, I took along a few medical supplies. I later disclosed this to the shaman along with the news that I had gone to medical school.

Seeing that my supplies included some medicine that could eradicate intestinal parasites, the shaman became excited. Children were dying from infections that his shamanic healings could not cure. He gratefully accepted my gift of medicine.

At that moment, everything fell into place. Medicine could be a healing practice when done and timed properly. It could be woven into a larger healing plan that could work with the individual's innate capacity to heal.

I returned from the jungle with a new perspective. I had ended my very short career as a doctor and begun my long career as a healer.

Psychiatry appealed to me because it seeks to help the mind, the most interesting part of being human, although also the source of so much of our pain. I hoped that in psychiatry I could learn how to help. I also was hopeful that my healing outlook would be tolerated by what seemed a relatively open-minded field of medicine.

My hopes proved well founded. In my psychiatry studies, the professors tolerated and even took an interest in my perspective. I had the green light to move ahead.

I soon realized, however, that if I were to help others to heal their minds, I would have to heal my own. If I didn't resolve my own issues, I could pollute and derail the healing of others. I understood the meaning of the phrase "Healer, heal thyself."

Plenty about me needed to be healed. I had scars on my skin from the physical violence I had endured in my youth, and scars on my spirit from childhood adversity. I took on the project of healing for my own good as well as for the good of those who would come to me for help. When you read here about the practices of enhancing and guiding healing, know that I have personally experienced most of them. I have bared my soul to many who have touched me deeply and have helped me immensely. Although I have not taken medicine, I know now that there were times when it would have made my journey safer, easier, and faster. Being able to prescribe medicine for others is a challenging blessing. I can see how powerfully helpful it can be for healing, but I'm also aware of how dangerous it can be and how it can interfere with the flow of healing when it's not used properly.

My own healing journey has been painful, comforting, arduous, and wonderful. It has successfully delivered me to a stage of comfort and confidence. It has shown me that healing is possible.

The many people who have come to see me in my practice over the years have taught me that the human spirit is strong, resilient, and capable of finding its way to wellness. With courage and perseverance, I trust that you will find your way as well. My deeply held hope is that *Mind Easing* will make your healing journey safer, more direct, and more effective. I've written this book because it matters very much to me that others might find their way out of suffering and into a life of greater ease.

Suggestions as You Read *Mind Easing*

- Be mindful that whatever you do to enhance, guide, or restore your healing is safe to yourself and others.
- Practice creating a personalized healing plan. If you are generally content, it may consist only of Layer One: Enhancement.

- If treatment is needed to guide or restore healing, discuss your plan with your therapist, prescriber, or other healing assistant.
- Most chapters end with a summary table to help you review and focus on the high points.
- Remain firm with the understanding that with persistence you will find your way to greater comfort.
- Consult with a professional if you are ever in doubt about what to do or if you feel overwhelmed by the task.
- This book should not be used to diagnose or treat emotional or mental suffering. Such activities should be overseen by a qualified professional. The purpose of this book is to help you keep the emphasis of wellness and treatment on healing.

CHAPTER 1

What's Your Healing Plan?

"Are you going to treat me, or are you going to help me to heal?"

"Are you going to do what's 'medically necessary' to justify your insurance claims, or are you going to do what's in the best interest of my wellness?"

"Will you help me find whatever approach is best suited for me, even if it does not include your services?"

*L*isa was interviewing me. She was trying to decide if she wanted to see me for help with her sadness and fears. And though she apologized for her bluntness, I applauded her courage and told her I shared some of her frustrations.

Many in the mental health treatment system have lost their way. They've lost sight of their purpose: to assist healing. I understand why. In the mad dash to find and provide relief, it's easy to disregard the concept of healing. Medicine is overprescribed because it works fast and saves health insurance dollars. Never mind that it can blunt your feelings and slow your thoughts. Never mind that it can result in serious side effects and derail healing. As long as enough of the people who take it can go to work and seem to function in their stressful lives, medicine will remain the popular solution.

Don't get me wrong. I'm in favor of using medicine when it's needed. I think it's foolish to ignore powerful medications that can save lives and restore healing. I also think it's foolish to overuse them and to use them in place of wellness promotion, psychotherapy, and other healing arts.

I told Lisa that I operate from a healing perspective and that I consider any treatment a way to assist that healing. Assisting healing, I said, is more likely than simple treatment to help without harming. It is also more likely to result in greater self-awareness and wisdom. I made some suggestions that I thought would help Lisa decide if she would be comfortable working with me. "It's time for you to stop being treated and start being healed. It's time to place whatever helpful approaches you choose within the context of a healing plan. It's time for you to insist that attention be given to healing as the driving force behind your recovery and wellness, and it's time for you to write your own healing plan. If you wish to work with me, I can help you with that."

Lisa decided we should continue on together, and throughout *Mind Easing*, she and I will share her healing plan as a way of helping you create one for yourself.

Your Healing Plan

Having awareness of how your mind heals itself from anxiety and depression, and helping it to find its own way, requires attention, humility, and flexibility. Sometimes the best way to help natural healing is by getting out of its way and simply witnessing its course of action. Though healing often needs help, what that help needs to be is not always clear. As healing unfolds and progresses, the ways you help it must be responsive and adaptive. It is wise to remain open to all possible avenues of healing, even if they seem odd and unfamiliar.

That's where a healing plan comes in. Unlike a treatment plan, a healing plan works directly with your natural healing process to enhance, guide, and restore your natural flow of healing to help resolve your distress and find your way to greater ease.

I'll show you how to work with your natural flow of healing instead of imposing hastily chosen treatments. You'll learn to make decisions about wellness, therapy, and medicine based on what would work best for your own unique style of healing.

The Three-Layered Healing Plan organizes a variety of helpful approaches in a way that best helps your mind to heal. The layers are organized by increasing need and intensity. You'll start with healthy attitudes and behaviors, and then you can add more intensive approaches like psychotherapy or medicine if they are needed—or remove them if they are unnecessary or causing more harm than good. I'll show you how to select the approaches that will best suit your needs and how to modify your plan as your recovery proceeds. The objective of the Three-Layered Healing Plan is to give healing what it needs so it can take care of you.

You might be tempted to jump to the highest layer of treatment (medicine) without realizing that a less intense approach may be as effective, promote lasting change, and produce the greatest long-term rewards. The risk of rushing too quickly into using medication is that it could hinder the natural flow of your healing by blunting your emotions. It could also expose you to unnecessary side effects. Using medicine when it's needed makes sense, but using it when other approaches may work as well does not. In *Mind Easing*, I try to help you decide if medicine is right for you, but you should discuss this with your own qualified professionals before you make your final decision. Making decisions that are consistent with your natural flow of healing will produce greater long-term as well as short-term rewards, whether those decisions include the use of medicine or not.

How to Assist Your Healing Plan

In Layer One: Enhancement, you'll learn how to use healthy attitudes, behaviors, and compassionate love to empower your natural healing process. In Layer Two: Guidance, you'll gently but firmly redirect the flow of healing with psychotherapy and other nonmedicinal treatments. Layer Three: Restoration includes medical treatment when necessary to remove severe, distracting, or disabling symptoms in order to reengage the flow of healing. With proper timing and skillful application, you can use these layers to synergize and complement one another while promoting your natural healing flow.

An effective healing plan incorporates as many of these three layers as are needed. It is not just a treatment plan, and it is not just a wellness plan; it is a comprehensive plan of wellness and, as needed, treatment that remains fully observant of and responsive to your unique healing style.

When things are going well and maintenance of a healthy resilient state is the goal, enhancement may be sufficient. If you feel like you are going the wrong way with distorted perceptions and unskillful behaviors, guidance may be needed. If you have symptoms of panic, obsession, or despair that are so severe that they distract or even block your capacity to take action to be well, medicine may reduce your symptoms enough to restore your flow of healing.

Let's now explore these three layers in more depth with Lisa's story guiding us.

Lisa's Story

"Stop! You're hurting me! That's too hard! You have to stop!"

Lisa awoke alone and crying in her Upper West Side condo. The siren on the street below punctuated her alarm.

She still thought of the prewar unit as her family's place even though she'd inherited it the previous year after her mother's long illness. She'd moved last summer from the family home on Long Island.

Padding across the floor through the shadows from the streetlights, she saw her reflection in the mirror. "Not bad for thirty-three. But why am I still alone? And why does my life suck?"

The nightmare that awoke her was recurrent, and she had no idea why it kept happening. Her cries also woke her dog, who sniffed the air and wagged her tail.

"What would I do without you, Ginger? You saved my life," Lisa said as she patted Ginger's head.

Actually, Lisa had saved Ginger from an animal shelter, after the dog had been beaten and abandoned. Ginger was the angel who entered Lisa's life five years ago, after her father had died suddenly. She had also comforted Lisa during her mother's battle with cancer.

As Lisa sat on the toilet, she said to Ginger, "Maybe Mother was right. Maybe I should get back into therapy."

Therapists and psychiatrists were decidedly not for Lisa. They had so far provided minimal comfort and no helpful suggestions. The medications she was given made her woozy and fat, and her last therapist had seemed bored.

But clearly she needed to do something. Try something.

⟿⟾

Lisa's friend Rachel had been seeing me for individual therapy and was also in my psychotherapy group. Rachel had come light years from the shattered soul who first walked in my door. She no longer needed medicine and was generally comfortable in her skin. I knew she'd be finished with psychotherapy soon.

Rachel asked me, "Would you please see my friend Lisa? I know you don't like to see people who are close, but we're just good friends, and I know you could help her!"

I said I would be glad to see her.

⟿⟾

When she arrived for her first appointment, Lisa was surprisingly timid. I knew that she owned a successful styling salon in Midtown Manhattan with several employees. She seemed pleasant and gracious, so why the scared rabbit, *I wondered.*

She was petite, stylish, and clearly uncomfortable. I asked her why.

"It's because I don't trust you."

"That makes sense," I said. "You don't know me."

I knew there must be more.

After some small talk, she told me about her disappointments with therapists and psychiatrists.

"Psychiatrists don't listen, and psychotherapists have their own agendas," she said. "Plus, antidepressants are toxic, and they don't do any good."

"Why did you decide to come see me?" I asked.

"I hoped you would be different."

That's when Lisa asked her hard questions about whether I would help her heal.

After we agreed to work together, Lisa revealed more. Her father was an alcoholic, worked long hours, and was prone to fits of rage. As a child, she was terrified that her father might hit her when he was drunk like he did her older brother. Lisa's father's alcoholism and rage contributed to Lisa's codependency. Because of her fear of being hurt and rejected, Lisa worried so much about what her father and others in her life thought of her that she had trouble identifying her own feelings and needs. Because of her fear-driven need to satisfy others, Lisa had lost track of herself.

Her mother kept up appearances and tried to hide Lisa from her father when he was angry. She took Lisa to dance lessons and got her a role in a commercial when she was ten. Lisa did some modeling in high school and struggled through cosmetology school. Her father helped her financially to start her business.

Meanwhile, there were significant family secrets. Her mother had tried—unsuccessfully—to hide her husband's drinking from the neighbors. When she was in high school, Lisa found a letter in the attic in which her mother's mother revealed that her grandfather had killed himself after he returned from the war. It wasn't a heart attack after all.

There was depression in the family that was very likely genetic. There was certainly plenty of distress.

Lisa broke down crying about her grandfather. "I never knew him," she sobbed. "I was just a baby when he died. I'm afraid I might be like him."

No wonder she'd previously been prescribed antidepressants. Lisa was profoundly depressed, and her anxiety was at times so severe that she had panic attacks and couldn't go to work.

I complimented her strength and courage and remarked about how hard it must be to carry around such fear and sadness with no one to go to for comfort.

"When my mother died, it was the last straw. She was my anchor."

Lisa was suffering greatly. Her anxiety was nearly unmanageable, and she felt very little enjoyment in her life. She was comforted by the thought that she could escape her pain by killing herself. She had nightmares but wouldn't tell me about them. Her concentration was so impaired that her bookkeeper had to pay her bills.

Lisa's death wishes were ruminative, and she assured me that she had no intent of harming herself. Still, there were faint scars on her left wrist, and I knew that her possible genetic depression could have been magnified by childhood adversity. Plus, there was plenty she wasn't saying.

"Look," I said, "unfortunately there's no blood test, genetic test, or imaging yet that will say for sure whether you're hurting because of genes or circumstances. So the best I can give you is an educated guess about what's causing your pain. It may be both your genetics and your upbringing combined with a stressful and lonely lifestyle. I think we should collaborate on a healing plan."

"Oh, good. You didn't say 'treatment plan.'"

"Right," I said. "Let's start thinking about what steps we can *take to help you heal. We should consider from the start what might be in the best interests of your long-range healing and growth, while also thinking of what might provide some short-term relief."*

Lisa wiped her tears and looked out the window at the gray day. "All right. What do you have in mind?"

We discussed how Lisa's initial healing plan was going to be temporary and focused on safety. First, she needed some tools to be able to stay alive, have a reason to live, and find some relief. Resolving childhood issues and relationship distortions would have to come later.

She remained firm in her resistance to medication. "I know it might help, but I've had some bad experiences and have very little faith."

She agreed to reconsider medication if her panic attacks and despair did not subside with lifestyle changes and therapy. She also agreed not to harm herself and to give a healing plan a real try.

Lisa's Initial Healing Plan

Given her busy life, lousy self-image, and resulting low self-esteem, my first suggestion was that we try to give Lisa an attitude adjustment.

"You're only looking at your flaws and failings because you are so sad. Your sadness gives you wrong ideas about yourself," I said.

Although I didn't yet understand all the aspects of Lisa's sadness, they seemed to include unfinished bereavement of her mother's death, the loss of her original family, some negative perceptions of herself from her childhood, and a possible genetic contribution.

"What matters," I said, "is that you see yourself as who you are: a beautiful person who is loving and loveable. You have a kind,

generous heart, and you have more strength and capability than you realize."

This was easy to say. I'd heard enough about her family, her friends, her dog, her business, and her various skills to know she deserved better than she was giving herself.

She agreed to try to see her strengths and not just focus on her weaknesses.

I went on to formulate a set of health-promoting actions with her. They included mindfulness, exercise, diet, and stress management (MEDS). She thought the acronym "MEDS" would help her remember our plan. I wrote it on a prescription pad.

"Will my health insurance cover this?" she asked.

"I don't know. It may be worth asking," I said. "Some insurance companies help with health club memberships and yoga classes."

We discussed the rest of the MEDS strategy. Fortunately, Lisa had had some experience with meditation. She had dropped her Pilates class but thought it had been good and was willing to return. Food was a challenge, especially because she lived alone, but she agreed to eliminate sugar, cut back on wheat, and reduce her alcohol consumption.

"It's okay," she said. "I'm so afraid of being an alcoholic that I hardly ever drink."

She'd had a run with cocaine, but this scared her and she had stopped. Shopping was an issue, but she hadn't had a bankruptcy and had no interest in gambling. She may have dodged the genetic bullet of addiction, but she used shopping as medication.

"I return things when I realize I bought too much," she said.

Having constructed Layer One of Lisa's healing plan, we went on to Layer Two.

My strongest concern for Lisa was that she stay alive and not hurt herself. I didn't want to nag her with my fears, but I wanted to be sure she would be safe.

The first task, then, was to create a safety plan—a plan for what she could do in the darkest moments when death seemed like the only way out.

I wrote on a card, "No matter how hopeless it may seem, things will get better." I explained that a human flaw is the belief that misery is permanent.

"You won't necessarily believe me when I say your misery will pass and things will get better," I said, "but I have seen a lot of people in states of profound misery, and things have always gotten better."

Abject misery, even though it feels permanent, does pass. The mind and the brain find ways to adapt and ways to see things in a different light. Feelings shift as time goes on.

Also on the card, we wrote names and phone numbers of people she could call if things got bad. We also added some positive reminders of her strengths and resources.

I went on to recommend she practice gratitude. "The exercise of gratitude is most helpful when you feel you have the least," I told her.

For now, I recommended we meet weekly. Later, I said, it may be helpful for her to do some group work and attend some self-help meetings, but because her fears and shyness were driven by something not yet revealed, my concern was that making herself vulnerable with strangers could be premature and set her back. She agreed to call if things got worse.

As for Layer Three, medical treatment would merit further discussion. Aside from Lisa's unwillingness, taking an antidepressant can, at first, occasionally lead to an increase in suicidal thoughts. When people start taking an antidepressant and it's effective, it sometimes results in greater energy and drive before there is relief of hopelessness. The risk then is that someone may be more likely to take action to harm herself if her energy improves before her mood. If Lisa were to decide on an antidepressant, I would review this risk with her and caution her to tolerate her misery until it went away. But I felt strongly that now was too soon to decide, and it seemed safer to wait.

Lisa said she would reconsider the use of medicine if her symptoms did not resolve with therapy and wellness enhancement (Layers One and Two). If her anxiety, panic, and despair continued to be extreme, they could block her capacity to help herself with those other means. That would be the time to revisit the medication option.

I did suggest, however, that she have some blood tests. I wanted to be sure we did not miss a simple medical problem that could mimic or worsen her symptoms.

I gave her a prescription for thyroid level, blood count, EKG, and basic kidney, liver, and electrolyte levels. I also checked blood sugar and wrote for a baseline set of cholesterol and triglyceride studies, in case any future medicine could cause a subsequent problem with sugars and fats.

Lisa seemed relieved and optimistic and said she would see me the following week.

Lisa's Initial Healing Plan

Layer One: Enhancement

Attitudes: Reinforce positive in-looks by reviewing strengths, essential goodness, and loving nature. Practice gratitude daily along with faith in the assisted course of healing.

Behaviors: **MEDS**

Mindfulness: At least 3 minutes of quiet meditation daily to still the mind. Frequent reminders to breathe and return to the moment with attention to what you are doing.

Exercise: At least 3 minutes of brisk exercise daily. Do not bother changing your clothes to do it. Resume weekly Pilates and yoga classes.

Diet: Avoid sugar and alcohol. Go light on wheat. Take Omega 3 fatty acids and have lots of vegetables.

Stress management: Resign from stressful volunteer work. When possible, commute at times when others are not. Maintain manageable work hours, spend less than you earn, and get enough sleep.

Compassionate Love: Spend more time with people who are kind and supportive and less with people who are negative.

Take Ginger [Lisa's dog] for long walks.

Layer Two: Guidance

Continue weekly supportive psychotherapy. Consider group therapy and self-help meetings later. Consider massage therapy and strengthen your spiritual program.

Layer Three: Restoration

Consider antidepressants if Layers One and Two do not reduce symptoms enough to permit constructive self-examination or if a suicide drive persists. Go for blood tests to rule out simple correctable problems such as hypothyroidism or anemia. Check blood sugar, cholesterol, triglycerides for baseline values.

Your Healing Plan

Your healing plan may not look like Lisa's, but it will be assembled the same way.

It starts with a set of attitudes and behaviors tailored to your needs. No matter how well you feel or how much you suffer, taking the time to assemble a set of healing enhancements is fundamental and necessary for an optimal healing plan.

If you had an easy and supportive childhood, and if you have not inherited a painful condition, Layer One: Enhancement may be all you need. It will help you take on and manage the stressful and disappointing events that life may throw at you. It will also improve your physical health and keep you alive longer.

If your childhood was anything like Lisa's, you may need some help making sense of it and lessening the grip it has on you now. Childhood as well as adulthood adversity and trauma can leave you with a set of distorted perceptions and responses. It can program you to expect the worst and to behave as if the worst is happening even if it isn't. Awareness and guidance to effect change can help. That's the task of Layer Two: Guidance.

You are fortunate to live at a time when many forms of guidance are available and when seeking them is acceptable. It is a sign of strength and courage to decide that you need some help understanding what went wrong and what you can do about it.

The most popular form of guidance in post-industrialized societies is conscious guidance. Various types of psychotherapy and counseling can help you examine what went wrong earlier in your life so that you can more clearly sort out what's right and wrong in your current life. A skillful therapist or counselor can then help you decide how to improve your relationships and lifestyle.

Some people seek guidance in nonverbal ways. Lisa plans to start with therapeutic massage. She might just as well have chosen yoga therapy, acupuncture, or other forms of body and energy work. Nonverbal forms of guidance like these can be powerful on their own, and they can boost the effect of conscious guidance when added to it.

Perhaps the world's most popular form of guidance is spiritual guidance. Whether through religion, in a twelve-step recovery program, or with the help of a pastoral counselor or shaman, spiritual guidance can be a lifesaver. If you can put yourself in a state of mind that invites a state of grace, healing will flow more powerfully and naturally.

Lisa's spiritual program includes meditation retreats, twelve-step recovery meetings for adult children of alcoholics, and walks on the beach. Yours may be more or less structured than Lisa's. Whatever spiritual path you may follow, if it includes having faith in your capacity to heal, it's likely to help.

If your path of healing becomes blocked and grinds to a halt because of overwhelming fear or despair, it may need to be restored. Sometimes suffering is greater than the capacity of guidance to help, and medicine may be needed.

Lisa was opposed to the use of medicine because of the side effects she had experienced. If her capacity to heal becomes incapacitated by panic or hopelessness, she may need to reconsider. Medicine often helps reduce suffering enough for progress to be made with therapy.

I did not want to push medicine on Lisa, and I don't want to push it on you. Although it can be valuable and even lifesaving, medicine can cause side effects that can be worse than the problem it's designed to help. It can also interfere with healing by brain blunting. It can flatten feelings and slow thinking so much that constructive guidance cannot do its job.

It's important to consider medicine carefully and to use it only when it's needed or when it's likely to help you heal. In Lisa's case, she may have inherited a condition that guidance may not be able to fix. Some conditions of the mind are hardened by genetics and biology. Think of them as neurological conditions. If your family members tend to suffer with severe depression or mood swings or panic, part of your suffering may be due to genetics.

With conditions of the mind, it can be hard to tell where the effects of genetics ends and those of adversity begin. Sometimes severe trauma and adversity can cause a hardened condition that, like a genetic one, does not respond easily to talk therapy or other kinds of guidance. Sometimes trauma becomes so engrained that it simply won't respond to words and deeds alone. That's when medicine can help. It can reduce symptoms enough for therapy to be effective.

If you don't have a genetic condition or a history of severe trauma or adversity, you may still benefit from medicine. Sometimes a highly stressful lifestyle is so overwhelming and distracting that it can be hard to make progress in therapy. If medicine helps you handle the stress without blunting your feelings, it might be worth considering.

In Lisa's case, I suspected she might have a genetic condition (genetic depression) as well as distress caused by childhood adversity and trauma. She may need and benefit from a carefully chosen and monitored medicine if her symptoms worsen and enhancement and guidance turn out not to be enough.

The beginning of Lisa's healing plan is fairly clear. It could change over time as her awareness deepens and events in her life change. Your process of constructing a healing plan may not be so clear. It can also feel scary.

You will not be alone as you assemble your healing plan. Lisa and I will help you find your way.

CHAPTER 2

Why You Suffer

Think about what's wrong before you try to fix it.

*I*f you want to heal safely and effectively, you'll need to have a good idea about why you are anxious or depressed. There's more than one possible cause of distress, and if you know what's causing your anxiety or depression you'll be better equipped to decide what to do about it.

The approaches you choose to assist your healing process should be the ones that will correct the *cause* of your anxiety or depression. Some approaches work well for some causes but they don't work well or even make things worse for others. There's no sense in barking up the wrong tree. Take some time to consider the three essential causes and the two mimicking causes of anxiety and depression.

The first major concept we discussed was the importance of using a comprehensive healing plan instead of a treatment plan. The second major concept to consider is the importance of basing your healing decisions on the causes of your anxiety or depression rather than their symptoms. This concept—basing healing decisions on the *causes* of anxiety and depression—is fundamental for a safe and effective healing plan. Both concepts run counter to the current standard practice of mental health care.

Standard Diagnostic Practice in Mental Health Treatment

Psychiatric diagnoses are currently based on symptoms rather than causes. If you have enough of the right symptoms, you qualify for a diagnosis that then has standardized treatment recommendations.

Here's an example: For a diagnosis of major depression using the current system of *DSM-5*, you need to have five or more of these nine symptoms:

- Depressed mood
- Lack of interest or pleasure
- Significant weight loss or gain
- Sleeping too much or too little
- Agitated movement
- Slow movement
- Fatigue
- Trouble concentrating
- Recurrent thoughts of death

If you have five or more of these symptoms and if they interfere with your work or love life, you qualify for a diagnosis of major depressive disorder. This ordinarily would lead to a recommendation for antidepressant medication.

Here's the problem: Those symptoms could have more than one cause, and the cause might not respond to the usual treatment recommendation. Let's say you're feeling down, not enjoying your life, your sleep is off, you've lost your appetite, and you're having trouble concentrating, but the reason you're upset is because you've overextended yourself at work, you're experiencing a relationship crisis, or someone you love just died. Unless your symptoms are truly disabling, taking an antidepressant might actually delay your healing if all you need is to talk it out. Taking medication could cause impaired concentration and blunted emotions that will interfere with your capacity to resolve the problem by less intensive means.

The point is that making a diagnosis without knowing its cause can send your healing plan in the wrong direction. If you pay attention to the cause or causes of your distress, the decisions you make about treatment are likely to be safer and more effective. If you and your treatment provider think you would benefit from an antidepressant because it could help you make better use of psychotherapy to resolve the issues that cause you to be depressed, then it might make sense to try it. If your depression appears to be due to a genetic condition that won't respond to therapy, then it makes sense to try it. But if you're using medicine to solve a relationship problem or a recent loss, it may do more harm than good. Medicine could blunt your emotions and divert your natural course of healing.

You probably already know if you are anxious or depressed, but do you know why? The answer to that is not as hard as you may think. There are three essential causes of anxiety or depression and two causes that mimic them.

The three essential causes of anxiety and depression are:

- Unreasonable stress
- Childhood adversity and trauma
- Genetics

The two causes that mimic them are:

- Medical problems
- Addiction

When I think about someone who struggles with anxiety or depression, I ask myself, *Why is this person nervous, scared, sad, or despairing?* By starting with this question and returning to it every time we meet, I keep my mind on the likely causes of that person's distress, which leads me to practical solutions. I recommend that you follow the same line of reasoning.

Since I think it's important not to bark up the wrong tree, I first rule out causes that could mimic the real reasons for anxiety or depression. I think of them as imposters because they can fool you into thinking the wrong way about what's wrong.

Medical Mimicry

The first imposter I rule out is medical mimicry. Here's an example: If you look and feel depressed because your thyroid hormone level is low, no amount of talk and no amount of antidepressant medication will help. A simple blood test will give you the answer. If your thyroid level is low and if you take supplemental thyroid hormone and feel better, you'll know that having an underactive thyroid was at least part of the cause of your depression.

Medical mimicry is important to consider for these two reasons:

- If there is an easily correctable problem, start there. It makes no sense to try to correct a medical cause of anxiety or depression with psychotherapy or psychiatric medication if a medical treatment would fix it.
- If a serious or dangerous medical condition is causing anxiety or depression, it should be discovered and treated sooner rather than later.

Most of the causes of medical mimicry can be ruled out with a few simple blood tests, such as a blood count to rule out anemia and blood sugar levels to rule out diabetes.

Several medical problems can mimic anxiety and depression. If you are concerned that you may have one, see your primary care provider or the relevant specialist to explore this further.

Examples of Medical Mimics

Common Medical Mimic	What They Could Cause
Hormonal	
hypothyroidism	depression, anxiety
hyperthyroidism	panic disorder
premenstrual syndrome (PMS)	depression, anxiety, irritability
premenstrual dysphoric disorder (PMDD)	suicidal thoughts, severe depression, and anxiety
pituitary adenoma	depression, mood fluctuation, anxiety
perimenopause	mood fluctuation
Infection	
common cold	depression
urinary tract infection	delirium (especially in elderly)

Common Medical Mimic	What They Could Cause
Infection *(continued)*	
Lyme disease	anxiety or depression
Cardiovascular	
arrhythmia	panic, anxiety
Cancer	
leukemia	panic attacks
pancreatic	depression
brain	anything
Neurological	
multiple sclerosis	depression, mania, panic attacks
Parkinson's disease	depression

Medical mimicry is a two-way street. Sometimes anxiety or depression can look like a physical illness. Perhaps the most dramatic example of this is panic disorder mimicking a heart attack.

Every emergency department clinician knows about this. Someone having a panic attack is terrified and often experiences chest pain along with shortness of breath. Suffocation, in fact, is the medical model for panic attack. Suffocation automatically induces panic, and people who are having panic attacks often fear they are dying. When chest pain accompanies a sensation of suffocation, it's hard not to think a heart attack is happening. Since it's better to be safe than sorry, emergency room doctors assume the worst until proven otherwise. An EKG and a series of blood tests determine whether you'll stay in the hospital or go home with a prescription for an antianxiety medication.

Addiction Mimicry

Over the years, I have been called on to sort out the causes of mental suffering when addiction may be involved. Because of my background in addiction treatment, I've had considerable exposure to addictions imitating mental illness. It led me to publish several papers and a textbook chapter about the overlap and confusion between addiction and mental health diagnosis and treatment.

Since nearly 50 percent of people who suffer with primary "essential" anxiety or depression also struggle with a chemical or behavioral (gambling, food, sex) addiction, it's not surprising that things can get confusing. To make matters worse, at least half of the people in active addiction have substantial secondary anxiety or depression that usually goes away within two weeks after stopping the addiction.

Addiction is not just about drugs and alcohol. It can involve behaviors as well. In order to be considered a behavioral addict, you would have to use the behavior so much that it causes problems in your life and craving when you try to avoid it. The craving must be strong enough to compel you to return to its use despite your wish to be free of it. You might experience withdrawal symptoms like sweating and insomnia when you stop participating in the behavior. This can be the case for any behavioral addiction, including eating, shopping, sex, gambling, or Internet compulsions.

What Caused Your Addiction?

Addiction to a substance or behavior can happen for three reasons:

- You inherited the problem.
- You used the substance or behavior to reduce your suffering and addiction took on a life of its own.

- Your recreational enjoyment became exaggerated to the point of craving.

Most of us self-medicate. We use alcohol, entertainment, shopping, exercise, food, and sex to relieve stress and to distract us from distress. Some of it is normal and healthy. If you rely on it too much, it can take on a life of its own and create its own problems. It's sometimes hard to tell when that happens, but most people have a good idea when they have gone too far.

When use of a recreational drug or of a behavior becomes addictive, problems arise. Your spouse or partner might become concerned or upset. Your friends might wonder what they should do. You could get fired, go bankrupt, get arrested for drunk driving, develop a medical problem from eating too much of the wrong thing, or get arrested for illegal sexual behavior.

Before that happens, addictive behavior can begin to haunt you. You may become anxious or panicky when you have trouble getting the substance or doing the behavior. You may become sad and depressed from the direct effect of the substance or behavior on your brain or from the problems addiction has created in your life.

You may then have trouble knowing how much your suffering is due to an essential cause of anxiety or depression versus how much the suffering may be due to the addictive substance or behavior you are using to try to feel better.

Fortunately, there is an easy way to find out: *Stop for at least two weeks.*

It takes at least two weeks for the effects of an addictive substance or behavior to wear off. That's when you will be able to tell if there's another problem. The worst of the anxiety or panic you may have felt as a result of using or not having the substance or behavior will be gone by then. Its direct effect will have largely faded, and the worst of withdrawal will have dissipated. Then you will know if that was the whole problem or if you have two problems: addiction *and* essential distress.

If you are not able to stop for at least two weeks, then what you thought was a way to ease your distress has become an additional cause of your distress.

Addiction is the great imitator when it comes to mental health symptoms. With addictive use of substances and behaviors, anything goes. So many neuroreceptors are fired up and so many neurotransmitters are fouled up that symptoms of anxiety, panic, and depression are the norm rather than the exception. It is so easy to confuse addiction with the essential causes of anxiety and depression that many people are mistakenly given medication when they should be given detox and twelve-step meetings.

Three Essential Causes
of Anxiety and Depression

Once you have eliminated medical illness and addiction as possible causes of your distress, you are left with the three essential causes of anxiety and depression.

Unreasonable Stress

Don't underestimate the power of stress. It's not an illness, but when it is severe and persistent it can cause illness. After ruling out medical and addiction mimicry, unreasonable stress is the first essential cause of anxiety and depression. When too much stress pushes you over the top, the degree of stress you experience can exceed your capacity to manage it. Your stress has then exceeded your stress threshold.

Your *stress threshold* is the point at which too much stress gives rise to symptoms of illness. Depending upon your Achilles heel (your physiologic weak point), you might develop acid reflux, low back pain, migraine headaches, panic attacks, or depression. Your stress threshold is your epigenetic trigger point: the point at which high levels of cortisol or circulating inflammatory factors cause unwanted genes to be expressed. If you experience too much stress for too long, you run the risk of switching on those genes. If you practice ways to relieve your stress, hopefully you'll switch those genes back off. Be mindful of your stress threshold because if you spend too much time above it, you run the risk of switching on genes that you may not be able to switch back off.

Fortunately, you have an early warning system; when you exceed your stress threshold, you feel physically tense and emotionally nervous or sad. When you've exceeded your stress threshold and you feel anxious or depressed, you'll need to reduce your stress. Ways to reduce stress include

- Saying no to unnecessary activities
- Avoiding unnecessary relationship drama at work and home
- Spending more time with kind people
- Avoiding sugar so that your energy and mood remain more level
- Exercising regularly
- Getting enough sleep
- Spending less than you earn
- Remembering to breathe and bring yourself back into the moment whenever possible

There's no guarantee that these steps will protect you from exceeding your stress threshold, but along with professional help, if needed, they will go a long way toward keeping you well.

Childhood Adversity and Trauma

People often make the mistake of thinking something is wrong with them when, in fact, something wrong happened *to* them. If you were subjected to trauma as a child or as an adult, that trauma can result in long-lasting anxiety or depression. The effects of childhood adversity can be so severe that they look just like a more permanent genetic form of clinical anxiety or depression. Don't be fooled by this. Healing can happen by using guidance in the form of psychotherapy, body or energy work, or spiritual guidance. It may take longer than you'd think or wish, but if you keep at it, you're likely to achieve partial or even complete and permanent relief of the worst of your distress.

It's shocking when a child is beaten or raped. Everyone knows it's wrong, and everyone knows that the terrible harm that has been done may never be fully resolved. It's also shocking when an adult becomes aware of having been raped or beaten as a child. She or he may have been afraid to say something. At the time, the child may not have even known the significance of what was being done. Later, however, with enough courage, encouragement, and guidance, the adult can declare that she or he was abused and that this was wrong.

Less shocking, but sometimes just as destructive, is when a child has been persistently criticized, degraded, or neglected. Such hurtful and destructive behavior could have come from a parent, bullying classmate, teacher, or coach. The erosive effect of pervasive criticism or neglect can be damaging for decades and require considerable therapy to resolve.

Organizing her view of herself around her father's criticism of her is what Lisa had to do. When her father came home drunk and unpredictably abusive or sloppily affectionate, Lisa's young mind tried to make sense of his behavior. As an adult, Lisa couldn't believe kind and loving statements from boyfriends and girlfriends. They always seemed fake or designed to soften her so that they could take advantage of her for sex or for social stature. Lisa tended to be attracted to boys and men who turned out to be unkind and emotionally withholding. She had subconsciously incorporated her father into her expectations about men and about some of her close friends. She was drawn to people who treated her as her father did. This contributed to Lisa's negative view of herself.

The result for Lisa was to simultaneously need and fear intimacy. The crushing effect to her self-esteem led to fear and alienation. The emptiness she felt at times led to despair. She could easily misread the intentions of others. She could miss a wonderful opportunity for a relationship with a kind person because kindness was unfamiliar and not to be trusted.

Given her circumstances, the resulting anxiety and depression were to be expected. Lisa's experience illustrates the suffering that can result from abuse. Fortunately, Lisa could see that the abuse she endured was wrong and that with compassion and guidance she could change her view of herself and her place in it. With awareness and change, she could see herself in a more positive light, and she could expect and find greater kindness and fulfillment in her relationships.

Genetics

It is still a surprise to me when I meet someone who simply has a genetic condition uncomplicated by childhood adversity or current stress. The most clearly inherited conditions have a particular quality and set of responses. These conditions appear to share four chromosome sites, two which regulate the flow of calcium into brain cells.[1] Conditions that appear to have a risk of genetic transmission include major depressive disorder ("clinical" depression), obsessive-compulsive disorder (OCD), panic disorder, alcoholism and other chemical and nonchemical addictions, bipolar disorder, and schizophrenia. Much of the study of the genetic transmission of psychiatric conditions is being conducted by the Psychiatric Genomics Consortium (PGC), which has five hundred investigators (scientists) from eighty institutions in twenty-five countries. Its aim is to use a lot of information to better link specific genes to specific conditions. Eventually, the hope is that clinicians will be able to tell how much of an influence genetics has on someone's psychiatric condition. Being able to determine how much of a role your genetics plays in your anxiety or depression can help clinicians determine what forms of treatment and what wellness approaches will help you.

Whenever someone comes to me for help, I ask if anyone in the family has had similar problems. Sometimes it seems like everyone in the family has depression, anxiety, or panic attacks. In Lisa's case, several people on her mother's side were clearly depressed, and Lisa's mother's father killed himself. I made a mental note to myself to track Lisa's depression and to remain aware of her risk for suicide.

If you are able to, ask your blood relatives if anyone genetically related to you has had the kind of anxiety or depression you are experiencing. Even if you think all your problems were caused by childhood adversity or unreasonable stress, it is good to know if your suffering has a possible genetic component. Since we currently do not have practical and dependable genetic tests for anxiety or depression, asking your relatives about it is the best way to find possible answers about family histories. The information could help you develop an effective healing plan.

Nature or Nurture?

Childhood adversity and adulthood stress can look so much like genetic depression and anxiety that telling them apart can be hard. In fact, epigenetic research shows how environmental stressors can activate genetic expression. With the right (or wrong) type and amount of stress, a quiet and otherwise unexpressed genetic condition can come alive. When gene activation happens, two problems can occur. One is genetic depression and the other is depression due to stress or adversity. To use a computer analogy, the genetic condition is a hardware problem and the trauma response is a software problem. Each can look like the other, and they can coexist.

Sorting out nature from nurture is important because they call for different treatment approaches. Pure genetic depression or anxiety does not need the type of relationship therapy that childhood adversity or adulthood trauma requires. Pure genetic depression usually responds to medicine and sometimes to cognitive behavioral therapy (CBT).

Understanding how much you were affected by parenting and how much you were affected by genes requires self-awareness and information gathering. As you unravel how much you were affected by genetics and how much by stress and adversity, you will expand your self-awareness and accelerate your healing.

Lisa and I have some ideas to share with you about unraveling the causes of your anxiety and depression. Here's how we determined the likely causes of Lisa's distress.

Why Lisa Suffers

Early in our work together, I reviewed the three essential causes and the two mimicking causes of anxiety and depression with Lisa.

She interrupted me and said, "Okay. I think I get it, but bear with me.

"The blood tests you had me do showed my thyroid levels were low, which may have explained some of my fatigue and sadness. In fact, I felt like I perked up a bit after taking low-dose thyroid medicine. And yes, I agree to have my bones checked for osteopenia since excessive doses of thyroid hormone can accelerate it.

"My low thyroid level partly mimicked depression, right?"

"Right," I said. "And it seemed to be confirmed by you feeling better after taking supplemental thyroid hormone."

"Yes, I get it. As for addiction mimicry, I know I have a problem with shopping. It's gotten me into trouble. I almost lost my business. The money panic I went through with worry about bankruptcy mimicked anxiety and panic."

"Right," I said, "and what about alcohol?"

"Okay," said Lisa, "I know I'm at risk genetically because of my father's side, but I really think I have it under control."

I reminded Lisa of her heavy use of cocaine in the past and how the same could easily happen with alcohol. She agreed to keep talking about it.

"So," said Lisa, "I seem to have had both imposters mimicking anxiety and depression, and I seem to have all three essential causes."

"How's that?" I asked.

"Well, as for number one, unreasonable stress, I seem to have plenty. My mother died. I'm single and don't want to be, and there's too much drama happening with my friends and employees. I feel like it has put me over the edge."

"I think it did," I said. "You exceeded your stress threshold, and it led to greater panic and despair."

"I'm glad we're working on that. Then there's the second essential cause of anxiety and depression: childhood adversity. I had plenty of that! My father was a rageful drunk who beat my brother and screamed at me. My mother was so preoccupied with him that she didn't have time for us. My boyfriend, Jake, was afraid of him, and we went through a terrible breakup. I think my childhood has affected how I see myself and might explain why intimacy is so hard."

"I agree," I said. "Those childhood experiences are like distorted lenses through which you see the world. You might not always experience people as they really are because you expect the worst and magnify small problems."

Lisa sat quietly for a moment.

"All right, well, that's tough to hear, and I don't know how much I buy it, but I understand the concept, and I'm willing to look at it."

"That's all I ask," I said.

"Lastly," said Lisa, "is number three: genetics. I say, how can you tell? There's no genetic test for depression or anxiety. I think you're just guessing."

"You're right," I said. "I am guessing, and I could be wrong, but on your mother's side you said her father was severely depressed after World War II. It could have been entirely due to PTSD (a reaction to combat trauma) but others in his family suffered depression, and I think you said his brother and his mother had ECT.* Your family history suggests genetic depression, and your limited response to therapy might suggest the same. I don't recommend jumping right into an antidepressant, but if you find you're not getting anywhere with enhancement and guidance alone, medicine might help."

"This does not sound easy," said Lisa. "The best I can say is, at least you have a short list of why I'm upset!"

How the Three Essential Causes of Anxiety and Depression Line Up with the Three Layers of Healing

Although there is overlap, the most relevant layer of healing needed for the corresponding essential cause is shown.

Three Essential Causes	Three Layers of Healing
Unreasonable stress	Enhancement (healthy behaviors)
Childhood adversity and trauma	Guidance (therapy)
Genetics	Restoration (medicine)

---

* Electroconvulsive therapy (ECT), which we discuss later in the book, was used more extensively for depression before antidepressants became available in the 1960s.

CHAPTER 3

How Your Mind Naturally Heals

You may give up on healing,
but healing will never give up on you.

You are not alone. *Everyone suffers.* Even those with the greatest emotional health and the most comfortable circumstances have times of hardship, loss, and insecurity. As a human you are blessed and cursed with the gift of self-awareness, which makes the beauty as well as the harshness of life undeniable. As a human you are destined for times of emotional upset.

Thankfully, you are also destined to heal. Your mind, like your body, is equipped with natural healing mechanisms that activate as they are needed. Just as your skin naturally heals from a cut, so does your mind naturally heal from a disappointment or a loss. You don't need to force healing to happen; it happens on its own.

Healing is a process that operates in you, continuously repairing you and restoring your function. From the moment of your conception until the moment of your death, your natural flow of healing works to keep you well. Healing has properties and ways of functioning that can be understood and described. To understand how to assist healing with the Three-Layered Healing Plan, it helps to understand how healing works on its own.

Why You Heal

The primary goal of healing is to restore function. It is by continuing to function properly that you can stay alive and thrive and help others do the same. When you suffer, restoration of function involves finding comfort and relief of the distraction caused by anxiety and depression. As you heal, your mind is eased and restored to optimal functioning.

When you suffer a loss, your mind heals by automatically moving through stages of grief without requiring your intention. When you are fearful, you naturally seek comfort and reassurance. When you have conflicts and confusion, your mind seeks answers. If you suffer an overwhelming trauma, your mind walls it off and lets you resolve it in manageable pieces. These are examples of how your mind naturally heals. Your inherent healing process never gives up on you—even if you want to give up on it.

Understanding how your mind naturally heals will help you understand how to assist it. The Three-Layered Healing Plan is designed to assist your natural healing process by strengthening it and helping it stay on track. Knowing why and how you heal will help you make the right choices about how to assist your natural flow of healing.

The Invisible Anatomy of Healing

Healing has two essential characteristics: power and pattern.

Power is the degree of strength that drives your healing process. It has been described in many cultures for thousands of years. Most commonly in Western cultures it is called *life force* or *vital energy*. In many Eastern cultures it is called *chi* or *qi*. Your life force is the energy that powers you and your flow of healing.

If you have a generally positive outlook, a good diet, get an adequate amount of exercise, manage your stress level effectively, and surround yourself with caring people, you're likely to have a strong life force with which to empower your flow of healing. These wellness-promoting activities are presented in Layer One: Enhancement. There you will find examples of wellness activities that will empower the natural flow of healing for your mind.

Practicing healthy attitudes and behaviors empowers your life force by improving blood flow, reducing inflammation, and giving you more energy. You'll learn in Layer One how scientific studies confirm the healing-empowering benefits of a healthy lifestyle.

Your life force or vital energy is the fuel that powers your natural flow of healing. The way healing flows, its *pattern*, is the second characteristic of healing.

The pattern of healing is describable and predictable. Patterns of healing kick in and take over when you are hurt and suffering. These patterns of healing happen naturally and spontaneously, but sometimes they need help to stay on track. Guiding your healing with therapy and restoring it when needed with medicine is how the Three-Layered Healing Plan keeps your healing on track.

Here's an example of physical healing: A cut in your skin follows a characteristic pattern of repair. Immune factors are mobilized to keep your cut from becoming infected. Fibrinogens and clotting factors stop the bleeding and knit the skin back together. As long as your cut is clean and your natural healing power is strong, your healing will successfully follow its natural pattern. If your cut is dirty, though, it may not heal well without your help. It needs your guidance through cleaning it and bandaging it. This is one example of how you can assist your natural flow of healing.

The same is true for your mind. You will naturally heal from a tragic loss if you allow yourself to feel sad and if you accept the kindness and love of others as you grieve. If, however, you try to ignore your pain, or if you try to cover it with too much alcohol or drugs, you will not heal well. By intentionally abstaining from emotion-numbing drugs and by expressing your feelings, you can keep your flow of healing on track. Just as cleaning a skin wound helps with healing, you can do things to guide your mind to optimally and naturally heal.

Your Natural Mind–Healing Abilities

The patterns your mind follows as it heals are innate. They automatically activate when you need them. If you suffer a loss, you automatically grieve. If you grow fearful or sad, you seek comfort and you seek reasons for your distress so that you can resolve it. If you are subjected to a trauma, your mind protects you from being overwhelmed by regulating how much awareness of the trauma you can accept.

The following eight mind-healing abilities are self-healing mechanisms I have observed during more than thirty years of practicing psychiatry. Most of them are self-evident, and some of these self-healing mechanisms have been described by others. Knowing about your mind's self-healing patterns will help you construct your healing plan because your Three-Layered Healing Plan will enhance, guide, and, if needed, restore the natural patterns of healing I'm about to describe.

Your Mind Seeks Comfort

When you feel fearful or sad, your mind automatically seeks sources of comfort to find relief. This is a way you protect yourself from feeling hopeless.

This form of self-protection keeps you from giving up. Finding comfort when you need it helps you continue to meet your basic needs for food, shelter, and protection.

Experiencing comfort from distress will help you face your problem with a fresh look and less desperation. By having a break from intense distress, you are more likely to approach the problem more rationally and less impulsively.

Some people prefer to comfort themselves in solitude with walks in nature, exercise, reading, eating, spiritual reflection, shopping, playing games, watching movies and shows, using alcohol or drugs, or masturbation. Some seek comfort in the company of others in spiritual fellowship, heart-to-heart talks, the camaraderie of sports or public meetings, dancing, or in shared drinking, drugging, and sex. All these activities and more can bring comfort and relief to a troubled mind.

Depending on your level of distress and your capacity to handle it, your sources of comfort may bring you pleasure or, if taken too far, may bring you pain. When taken too far, some of these comforts can cause addiction (which comes with its own set of problems) or they can cause problems for a relationship or a job or with the law. When you feel desperate, the risk of making unhealthy choices is at its highest. The urge to escape the pain of anxiety and depression can be so strong that bad judgments regarding food, sex, shopping, alcohol, and drugs can lead to greater problems than the original causes of fear and sadness. Overuse of substances or behaviors can cause some people to become locked into an addictive spiral or result in legal, occupational, health, or relationship crises.

You must exercise restraint when your mind seeks comfort. Moderation is the key. If you're worried that you may have gone too far with comfort seeking, you probably have. Reach out to people who care about you, and tell them you fear you might go too far if you persist on a path that avoids pain but could result in disaster. If you can't moderate your use of comforting substances (like alcohol or drugs, including addictive prescription medicines), or if you can't moderate your use of unhealthy behaviors (like binging on gambling, shopping, or unhealthy food or sex), then you should stop. If you can't stop, ask for help right away. See the Addiction Counseling section of chapter 7 for more about help for addiction. When your mind automatically seeks comfort, you must remain vigilant so that it doesn't drive you into an active addiction.

Your Mind Seeks to Understand

We are an inquisitive species. We like to know why and how things happen. We like to know how things work and how to fix them when they break. Our inquisitive nature compels us to understand why we have fears and sadness, and how we can relieve our distress.

When we are in pain we seek the cause of our pain so that we can relieve it. Having the intellectual capacity to examine and understand the causes of pain and suffering is one of our greatest gifts. It has led to advances in medicine, including mental health treatment.

As you consider the cause of your emotional pain, you may ask yourself, *Is my relationship unhealthy for me? Do I keep choosing the wrong kind of person as a partner or friend? Could my boss be too demanding, or are my coworkers unreasonable? Am I trying to accomplish too much with too little time? Am I depressed because I haven't worked through my childhood disappointments? Did I inherit genes that cause depression or panic?*

As you ponder questions like these, you are likely to seek solutions to your distress. You may then ask yourself questions like these: *Should I say no more often? Do I need to be more tolerant of my partner's eccentricities? Should I look for another job or a different community or a different climate? Should I talk to someone about my childhood adversity?*

Your mind seeks reasons for your distress and ways to make it go away. Sometimes your mind might work so hard to find answers that the very process of self-reflection can become a source of pain. Just as I advised moderation in seeking comfort, I advise the same for seeking answers. Intellectualizing your distress to find ways to resolve it can be helpful, but it can also plunge you into a frustrating, ruminative loop of questions without answers. That's when it's time to stop thinking and start feeling.

Your Mind Feels Its Way to Wellness

Your mind, by nature, tends to feel what it needs to feel to be well. A healthy mind, unfettered by stress, childhood adversity, or bad genes will feel fear and sadness as it's meant to—and having those feelings leads to their resolution.

If you have been subjected to undue stress, childhood adversity, or unhealthy genes, you might find it difficult to know what you're feeling and whether your feelings are valid. You might not trust your feelings to be true. There is, however, no greater truth than what you are feeling in the moment. No matter the reason for what you're feeling—even if it's illogical—knowing how you feel and allowing that feeling to exist is a starting point for healing.

When people struggle to deny their feelings, their discomfort intensifies. Suppressing feelings leads to greater anxiety. When you deny that you feel scared, sad, mad, or glad, you start to feel that something's wrong, but you can't tell what it is. This does not mean you should act on your feelings. It may be in your best interest to delay expressing your anger until you understand the reason you feel angry and what would be the most constructive and least destructive way to express it. Similarly, impulsively expressing fear or sadness might put you at a disadvantage. It may be prudent to reflect on why you're scared or sad and how to safely and effectively ask for help.

If you are confused by your feelings and can't tell what they are, I recommend you ask yourself, *What am I feeling in this moment?* Even if you don't like how you feel or if you think your feeling is inappropriate, it's still how you're feeling. Identify your feeling and allow it to run its course.

Knowing and accepting how you feel will help you be more present and authentic. If you wish to be good company for yourself and for those around you, being honest with yourself about how you feel will lead to more genuine responses and actions.

People I work with in therapy often tell me, "I know I shouldn't feel this way." That's when I interrupt and say, "You may not choose to act on your feeling, but it's important to acknowledge the feeling so that it does not become bottled up and because it is the truth of how you're feeling in the moment. If you deny your feeling, you may become confused and anxious and respond to the feeling in ways that are unconscious and inauthentic."

If, in the context of a relationship with someone, you worry that you cannot safely or skillfully express a feeling to that person, give yourself some time to reflect on the feeling and consider whether and how to express it. If you're able to acknowledge the feeling to yourself and if you give yourself some time to consider its importance, you'll be better able to decide if expressing the feeling will be constructive or destructive to the relationship. If, after deliberate reflection, you have good reason to express your fear, sadness, anger, or other feeling, you're likely to find a way to do so that is not impulsive and is likely to promote better understanding and closeness.

If you're still not clear about what you're feeling or how to express your feelings, a therapist can help. A therapist has the advantage of objectivity and experience. A skillful therapist can help you identify your feelings, work through them by expressing them in therapy, and devise skillful ways of expressing them to the people in your life.

Your Mind Adjusts to Change

The capacity of your mind to adjust to changes in your life is astonishing. Your mind incorporates and adjusts to changes daily. Many of the circumstances you face, like traffic jams or rescheduled meetings, can be annoying, but they are relatively inconsequential. You may not even know that your mind is successfully working on them. During a typical day, you adjust to changes in temperature, weather, and social dynamics. You manage most sad news and glad news without missing a beat. It's the bigger, scarier issues that can challenge your mind's capacity to cope.

Every change in your life, big or small and welcomed or not, represents a gain or a loss—or both. Your mind automatically grieves losses, adjusts to gains, and incorporates the change by reordering how to see yourself and how you believe others see you. As your mind grapples with expected and unexpected changes, it automatically reorders your understanding of your world and it automatically adjusts how you respond to those changes now and in the future.

When you get a piece of news that is upsetting but not traumatizing, your mind does the best it can to accept it. Your mind assesses the bad news and compares it to issues it has handled in the past. If the current issue seems as manageable as previous problems, your mind may handle and incorporate the information with no struggle. If the information seems too upsetting to accept, your mind may decide to put it aside and go back to it at a calmer moment.

Once the information is processed and accepted, it is time for action. If the issue is important or requires your involvement to resolve it, your mind will urge you to take action. If the issue is a medical problem, the action may involve seeking more information. If the issue is a job loss, the action may involve networking and revising your résumé. A bigger issue may require decisions about where to live or how to live differently. Whatever decision you make, your mind will adapt to it.

Your mind will find ways to organize itself around the actions you take. It will rearrange your perception of yourself and your place in the world. It will help you make sense of the change that has happened, and it will prepare you for the consequences of your decision or action.

Your Mind Knows How to Grieve

Just as your mind will lead you to seek love and make attachments, it will help you to let go of them when they are over. You have the capacity to love and to bond. It is part of seeking comfort, and it is part of what you need to survive and to thrive. As a social creature, you need others for safety, comfort, and joy. When your attachments come to an end because of death or separation, your mind comes to your rescue with the capacity to grieve.

Among the many people who have studied grieving was Elizabeth Kübler-Ross, a Swiss-trained psychiatrist who worked in Chicago. In her book *On Death and Dying*,[2] she describes the five stages of dealing with death: (1) denial and isolation, (2) anger, (3) bargaining, (4) depression, and (5) acceptance. These stages of grief don't always happen, and they don't always follow the same order, but they usually occur at some point following an important loss. Dr. Kübler-Ross gave us a way to understand and anticipate how our minds usually heal following the loss of someone or something important to us.

In my work with people who are grieving, I've found that everyone has their own grieving process and everyone grieves at their own pace. Although Dr. Kübler-Ross's stages of grief describe the experience of many people, some start with shock and disbelief and proceed directly to gut-wrenching sobbing; others accept the news stoically and push down their feelings until they can have some time alone. Some people are surprised they don't feel much and wonder if they're grieving the right way.

As long as you don't drown your feelings with alcohol or other forms of addiction, and as long as you don't harm others if you feel outrage, grieving happens naturally and spontaneously and eventually ends, for most, with occasional twinges of sentimental sadness.

Grief lasts longer for most people than they think it will. It also lasts longer for many than the people around them think it should. Sometimes friends and loved ones grow alarmed by the duration of grief of someone close to them. My advice to those who grieve is to tell people, "This may take longer than you may think it should, but it is, unfortunately, necessary for me to be very sad for a long time."

Your Mind Copes with Trauma

After decades of work with people who have suffered severe trauma in childhood and/or in adulthood, I have observed that trauma in the form of abuse by another person—especially someone familiar—usually has a stronger effect than trauma that was accidental or due to natural causes. In the case of childhood abuse, when the child knew the abuse was wrong, that child has an easier time recovering than a child who couldn't tell that the abuse was right or wrong. Early childhood trauma has a different character from adult trauma, but both need acknowledgment and release.

The mind's response to trauma is both comforting and troubling. When faced with overwhelming trauma, your mind can and will tolerate only so much. Your mind has a clever mechanism that shuts off awareness of trauma and thereby diminishes trauma's immediate effect.

Your mind's response to trauma is similar to how your body responds to infection. Sometimes a local infection is so severe that, try as it might, the body cannot fight it off. It's too overwhelming. In response, the body walls it off and forms an abscess. It contains the damage so that the infection will not destroy the organism.

Similarly, your mind can use denial to wall off an overwhelming trauma so that you do not go insane or do something stupid. Denial can protect you from incapacitation by severe distress or death from suicide. The problem is that the memory of a severe trauma can remain encased in your mind like a psychological abscess. A physical abscess can cause persistent inflammation and debilitation. A trauma memory, walled off by denial, can cause persistent fear and self-doubt that can erode your self-esteem and the quality of your relationships.

The solution for an abscess is easy: incision and drainage. We can't do that yet for walled-off trauma. It has to be released gradually with care and support. Go too fast and your mind can panic or become despairing, and make bad decisions like using addictive substances or unhealthy behaviors. Go too slow and your quality of life can be persistently degraded. Coaxing the mind to release its self-protective hold on trauma requires skill and compassion. For help with this, you may wish to engage a therapist who specializes in trauma resolution.

Your Mind Acquires Wisdom from Hardship

It's likely that you've already endured and survived significant hardship. Eventually, everyone experiences adversity and loss and suffers fears, disappointment, and sadness. You may have suffered so much misery that you wondered how you could possibly manage to survive.

Living a life devoid of hardship, unfortunately, is not possible. Knowing you can survive painful times and carry on with a deeper appreciation of your resilience and strengths is possible when you do not try to avoid hardship. If you do not try to escape the pain of hardship with too much alcohol, drugs, or medicine, you will gain resilience.

By enduring and surviving hardship, you know you can do it again if you must. You know that, no matter how bad your situation may be, it will eventually resolve or you will find a way to adjust to it. Knowing that you can endure hardship and adapt to it provides wisdom you can bring to future difficult times.

When you endure hardship, you usually acquire greater awareness of its cause. Since most of us tend to repeat unhealthy choices that lead to hardship, you're likely to eventually become aware of your own patterns of unhealthy choices. This will help you discover whom to avoid, when to say yes and when to say no, and how to find love and work that best suits you. By experiencing hardship from unhealthy choices, you gradually acquire wisdom to know what's right for you.

As you find your way through painful and pleasurable times in life, you also learn how to better enjoy the good times and better cope with bad times. Acquiring wisdom about how to safely manage pain and enjoy pleasure will help you construct a safe and effective healing plan.

Acquiring wisdom from hardship allows you to help others as well as yourself. The children in your life as well as your friends, relatives, lovers, and coworkers can benefit from your wisdom. When they are confronted with a dilemma similar to yours, you can share with them how you managed your hardship. This may help them make better choices for themselves. Be careful, however, not to tell them what to do. Their experience and how they handle it is different from yours. By sharing with them how you handled your own hardships, you give them ideas, and, more important, hope that they can handle their own difficulties.

Your Mind Seeks Help

We need each other, and we naturally turn to others for help when we need it.

We started life as helpless, though adorable, little creatures, and we had to be cared for by others in order to survive. When we were hungry, tired, or hurt, caring adults came to our rescue. We learned right away that others could help us when we were unable to help ourselves.

When you find yourself mired in anxiety or sadness and your natural self-healing mechanisms are not working well enough on their own, it's important to reach out for help. There's no shame in it. According to the Harvard Medical School National Comorbidity Survey,[3] having a diagnosable anxiety or mood disorder, including depression, happens to more than 50 percent of U.S. adults at some time in their lives, and no one manages to get through life without times of hardship, loss, and struggle with distress.

When your mind is overwhelmed and not managing to overcome anxiety or depression, many caring and qualified people are available to help. Just as it is in our nature to reach out for help, it is also in our nature to come to the help of others. Those who follow this calling as wellness instructors, therapists, and prescribers have a natural urge to care and to help. As you read about the Three-Layered Healing Plan, you'll learn how to construct your own plan, tailored to your unique style and needs, and I'll tell you what helpers to seek when you put your plan into action.

Lisa's Confusion

Lisa interrupted my soliloquy, saying, "If my mind is so relentlessly healing itself, why am I still feeling so empty and conflicted?"

"Your healing process hasn't let you down," I said. "It keeps trying to help you make sense of things. By reasoning, it struggles to understand what made you upset. By urging you to express your feelings, it helps you get through them and let them go. Your natural flow of healing hasn't let you down, but it could use some help.

"One way your mind has already accomplished a great deal of self-healing was by grieving your mother's death. When your mother died, your mind naturally grieved."

"I couldn't believe it when my mother died. Even though it was not a surprise, it was a terrible shock. I can still see her in the hospital bed with tubes and beeping machines. I knew it would happen. I just wasn't ready for it."

"No one really is," I said. "When someone so close to you dies, the finality is a shock. It's especially hard if the person who dies was kind to you. Mourning a kind, loving person takes a lot of time and energy."

"It's taking me so long that I'm starting to worry. My friends think I should be over my mother's death by now."

"Your grieving has its own schedule. You were very close to your mother. She tried to protect you from your father's rages, and she came through for you when you needed her love and support. It takes a long time to reconstitute after such a loss. As you grieve, your resilience will grow."

"But I feel so empty," Lisa whispered. Her eyes were downcast.

"That's natural with grieving," I said. "And it's complicated by the fact that you did not get enough love and kindness growing up."

"But I know they loved me," she whispered.

"Yes, from what you've told me, it's clear that they loved you, but your parents were distracted by your father's drinking and your mother's worries about him. They were also distracted by money and their urge to be successful. Their lack of attention to you and your needs affected your feelings about yourself and how you love."

"What's the difference between my mind trying to heal my grief and my mind feeling empty?"

"*The difference*," I said, "*is that your emptiness is deeper and more complicated than your grief. You feel empty when you miss the affection you never had. You feel grief when you miss the affection you did have. Healing emptiness requires an understanding of what was missing, and it requires effort to fill your needs with your current capabilities and resources. You have strengths and resources as an adult that you lacked as a child. By discovering and using your strengths and resources you will diminish your emptiness.*"

"*What can I do to help heal my emptiness?*" Lisa asked.

"*I recommend you start with supportive, insight-oriented therapy to clarify what happened to you in your childhood, to help you understand it was not your fault, and to help you express your feelings about it. Therapy will also help you find healthy ways to cope with the painful feelings you have and how to better manage your relationships with the important people in your life.*"

"*Isn't it enough just to know what happened to me?*"

"*Unfortunately, it's not,*" I said. "*Your thoughts can help with understanding why you feel the way you do, but you'll need to express and work through those feelings so that they won't cause you so much pain.*

"*Because you are bright, determined, and courageous, you will be able to resolve your childhood issues with therapy. Therapy will help you understand and accept more about yourself and it will help you let go of old unhealthy perceptions and responses and replace them with healthier ones. Your mind's natural capacity to heal will, with the help of therapy, help you find your way.*"

Your Natural Mind-Healing Abilities

- Your mind seeks comfort.
- Your mind seeks to understand.
- Your mind feels its way to wellness.
- Your mind adjusts to change.
- Your mind knows how to grieve.
- Your mind copes with trauma.
- Your mind acquires wisdom from hardship.
- Your mind seeks help.

How the Three-Layered Healing Plan Assists Healing

Characteristics of Healing	Layers of Assistance
Power	Layer One: Enhancement strengthens life force.
Pattern	Layer Two: Guidance keeps healing on track— and . . . Layer Three: Restoration brings healing back on track when it derails or becomes blocked.

Layer One

Enhancement

A few small lifestyle changes could make a huge difference in how you feel. The ABCs of healing enhancement—positive attitudes, healthy behaviors, and compassionate love—may be all you'll need to resolve your anxiety or depression. If they're not enough, they'll create a strong foundation for Layer Two: Guidance and, if needed, Layer Three: Restoration. When you combine an effective Layer One wellness plan with therapy and medicine, you're more likely to experience a good outcome. In addition, Layer One's healing enhancements will help your body as well as your mind. You'll be stronger and healthier as you resolve your emotional distress.

CHAPTER 4

Attitude Adjustment

Changing your in-look can brighten your outlook.

A ttitude is the A of the ABCs of healing enhancement. When combined with *behavioral change* and *compassionate love*, they form the most fundamental and enduring layer of a well-constructed healing plan.

For some, healing enhancements are the only things needed to reduce anxiety and depression to a manageable level. For others, healing enhancements provide a solid base to empower the healing effects of Layer Two: Guidance (with therapy) and Layer Three: Restoration (with medicine). Attitude adjustment is the starting point for healing anxiety and depression. Having a set of positive healing attitudes will help you take on your world and find your way to greater ease. The three healing attitudes I recommend you practice are self-acceptance, perseverance, and gratitude. Keeping these attitudes in good trim, even when times are tough, will help you maintain balance as you proceed toward your healing goals.

I learned an unforgettable lesson about proper attitude from my flight instructor. Martin was a fighter pilot who'd flown in actual combat dogfights. Martin taught flying at an isolated airstrip in the Appalachian Mountains. His airplane had two seats, one in front of the other. I was required to sit in the front seat.

Martin told me I must maintain proper attitude when flying. Attitude, a technical term in flying, means keeping your aircraft parallel to the ground so that as you fly toward the horizon you do not fly too high and stall or too low and crash into the ground. For my lesson in proper flying attitude, Martin required me to fly upside down.

His airplane was aerobatic, meaning acrobatic in the air. Like the fighter planes he flew in dogfights, his personal airplane could do loops and barrel rolls.

Flying upside down was not easy. The change fell out of my pockets, my sinuses became congested, and it was hard to breathe. Keeping an airplane parallel to the ground is hard when you're worried about your glasses falling off.

"Why do I have to fly upside down?" I asked him.

"If you maintain proper attitude upside down, it will be easier for you to do it right side up," was his answer.

This lesson helped me years later when a series of traumatic events happened while I was under extraordinary pressure to perform well academically. I remembered Martin's lesson about maintaining proper attitude. Keeping yourself in proper attitude is especially important when your life has turned upside down.

In flying, there are three attitudes: pitch, bank, and yaw. Proper pitch means not angling too high or too low. Bank means keeping your wings level so that you don't veer off course, and yaw means flying straight ahead instead of sideways. It's important to maintain all three attitudes so that you don't go the wrong way. In life, as in flying, it's easy to get thrown off course by unexpected turbulence. The lessons I learned about maintaining proper attitude while flying serve me well when I must maintain proper attitude in life, especially when life becomes stormy.

Three life attitudes will keep your healing headed in the right direction. Self-acceptance will strengthen you, perseverance will keep you going when you feel like giving up, and gratitude will give you reason to continue. If you can maintain these three positive attitudes, you will be less likely to stall, crash and burn, or veer off course.

Self-Acceptance

Accept all the ways you are with compassion
and loving-kindness.

It's normal to worry about measuring up. Most of us worry about how we look, what we wear, and where we live, and that we won't be good enough. It's in our nature to worry about being accepted and desired. We worry about being good enough even though that worry is unnecessary. As Muhammad Ali, the world-champion heavyweight boxer, said, "There's always someone bigger, better, and faster."

But beyond that, most of us fear we will be criticized or abandoned because of our self-perceived inadequacies. Our insecurities intrude in dating, job searches, and friendships. When we fear we are not good enough, we become anxious and lose self-confidence.

Persistent worry and self-perceived inadequacy can lead to feeling worthless. Persistent self-doubt erodes self-esteem and can lead to feelings of worthlessness and ultimately depression.

There are plenty of reasons for self-doubt and low self-esteem. Harsh criticism or cold neglect in childhood, traumatic experiences or unreasonable demands in adulthood, or a bad set of genes can all result in self-defeating beliefs.

No matter the cause, feeling inadequate or unworthy is an erroneous belief that can be changed. I have never known a person who deep down wasn't truly kind, well meaning, acceptable, and loveable. Even the most hardheaded bullies I've met were, underneath their bravado, simply afraid of being criticized and rejected. Even they could learn how to love and be loved without inviting the rejection they fear.

If you believe you are not good enough or loveable enough or that you fall short in some other way, here are two tools that may help you:

- Kill your shame with curiosity.
- Practice self-acceptance.

These tools will help you nurture the self-acceptance you need. Self-acceptance is crucial for healing your anxiety and depression. It strengthens your self-confidence and deepens your self-awareness. Self-acceptance relieves you of the burden of having to pretend to be someone you are not. It sets you free to define and follow your healing plan according to what you believe will work best for you.

Kill Your Shame with Curiosity

To stop judging yourself and start seeing yourself as you are, you'll need to develop your curiosity. If you are curious about what you feel, what you think, and how you behave, you are more likely to view yourself objectively and less likely to judge yourself unkindly.

You may have been raised in a family and in a culture full of expectations. You may have been expected to have been beautiful, intelligent, goal-achieving, outgoing, physically adept, or noteworthy. You may have been judged by your physical characteristics and accomplishments. You may not have been recognized or accepted as the unique and good person you are.

If this describes your experience growing up, there's a good chance you felt inadequate and misjudged. You may have grown up feeling that the people around you tried to understand you but didn't really know who you were. As a result, you may wonder who you are now.

As a child, you may have learned some destructive beliefs about yourself. This may have led you to feel unloved and unlovable. It probably created a harsh critic in your head. Your inner critic can judge your every look, your every move, and your every thought and feeling. It can teach you to see yourself as flawed and unworthy.

You can eliminate those learned intolerances with curiosity. If you can be curious about yourself and find yourself interesting, you will take some of the hurt out of old, shameful messages. Maintaining objectivity about yourself reduces shame and allows truth. If you can be curious about yourself, you will have greater compassion for yourself and you are likely to find yourself interesting and enjoyable. You can become your own best friend.

We are all imperfect creatures because of our nature and our upbringing. We all have flaws, and we do the best we can to find our way through life. Being curious rather than judgmental will help you accept yourself as you are and practice greater compassion and kindness in the process.

Practice Self-Acceptance

Curiosity in place of criticism helps self-acceptance, but it's only part of the story. If you want to replace your judge and jury with kinder messages to yourself, you'll have to practice accepting who you are. Here's how to help that process:

Every time you have a negative thought about yourself, replace it with a positive one. Every time. Don't give your judge and jury an inch. They need to be vaporized.

If you're like most of the people reading this, you won't have to wait long for some self-criticism. Negative messages were instilled at a young age and were reinforced by harsh parents, strict teachers, competitive classmates, and random mean people. Those criticisms accumulated and caused you to hold yourself in low regard. Don't let them have that effect on you. Those old messages are your judge and jury, and it's time to drive them out. They don't belong there. You don't have to believe them, and you don't have to listen. Drown them out with self-acceptance.

You are kind. You are good. You are strong. You have a beautiful heart. There are many things you do very well. You have acquired much wisdom. You have been underestimated and underappreciated. It's time to stop your negative beliefs about yourself.

During a codependency workshop retreat, Lisa was terrified by a requirement the leader made of her. She was told she must stand on a chair in front of ten people and say good things about herself for sixty seconds. She started to sweat, and her heart raced. Her hands were cold even though the room was warm. Her mouth was dry, and she wanted to disappear.

She had no choice. She was there for a reason. She wanted to get rid of her harmful self-criticism. She started by saying, "I think I'm an okay person." She was asked to say it with more conviction. "I'm a good person," she said nervously. "I care about people, I'm smart, I'm creative, and I'm strong. I love animals, and I love people. I'm good at running my business . . . and I'm a good swimmer." Lisa managed through fears and tears to acknowledge some goodness within herself.

Replacing unhealthy thoughts with healthy thoughts is nothing new, but it's something many of us forget to do. It works, and you can do it. Whenever you think a thought that's negative, replace it with a positive one. You'll have to be relentless and persistent. Your inner critic is well embedded and strongly reinforced, but you can change that with compassion and kindness for yourself.

Perseverance

> *If you're going through hell, keep going.*
> —Winston Churchill

Sometimes you just have to keep going even though you don't want to. I think of perseverance as a big bowl of determination filled with patience with a generous topping of faith. You've already persevered through stress, trauma, and tragedy. Now it is time for you to persevere through healing. Since you've already shown you could persevere when things were bad, you can know that you have the capacity to persevere as things get better.

Let's look at the three components of perseverance: determination, patience, and faith.

Determination

Things change. They always do. If you keep your mind on healing, things will change for the better. Sometimes it takes grit and determination to get there. Determination is an essential feature of perseverance. It's what you'll need to carry on.

Many things in life are harder and take longer than would seem necessary, and healing the mind can be one of them. Fortunately, most mind healing and personal growth takes place without your awareness. Nature takes its course and naturally resolves conflicts, increases your awareness, and deepens your wisdom with relatively little effort.

Sometimes, however, the business of natural healing slows, grinds to a near halt, or requires more of your attention and effort than you would like. That's when you'll need to be determined.

Years ago, during a workshop about surviving childhood abuse, I overheard the woman next to me muttering something over and over. During a break I asked her what she was saying.

She said, "Keep going. Keep going. Keep going. Don't give up, keep going." She told me she uses it as a mantra, repeating it over and over when times in her life are especially hard. She told me it helps keep her alive during her darkest times. She said that after hearing my personal story, she thought her mantra might help me during some of my darkest hours. I thanked her and told her there was no doubt I would find it useful.

Patience

Patience invites you to let go and accept the present while you wait for better times.

There is no greater truth than how you feel in the present moment. It is the only reality worthy of your full attention. No matter how painful it may be or how pleasurable it may be, it's all you have. It is this reality that will heal your mind. Having patience allows you to join with the reality of your life.

With patience comes acceptance of the moment. Patience helps you stay in the moment, and it will help you continue your course of healing. When you stay in the moment and accept how you feel, you allow it to pass. When you patiently stay with your healing plan, you give it a chance to work for you.

The best way to tolerate a desperate or frenetic time is by slowing down and waiting. Are you feeling rushed and desperate? Stop and breathe. Notice that you are alive while the world goes on around you. In fact, notice that you can slow down and wait in this very moment. When you slow down and breathe and stop forcing things to happen, they flow more smoothly and you feel less desperate.

Lisa's Impatience

Lisa was not patient. She wanted to be fixed. Now! She was entirely intolerant of her anxiety and depression because she found them painful, time-consuming, and completely without merit. As far as she was concerned, they had no right to take up so much space in her head.

Lisa suffered from bouts of severe anxiety, which she found at times incapacitating and intolerable. This led to her feeling hopeless. She had friends, family, and colleagues who were concerned and supportive. They encouraged her to seek treatment.

Several therapists and psychiatrists later, she found me. By then, in addition to being impatient, she was frustrated.

"Your distress and frustration with your anxiety are completely understandable," I said. "The problem is that several talented and

well-intentioned people have tried to help you, and they have not felt satisfactory to you."

"I know. That's why I came to see you! You've got to do something."

"In my opinion, more important than trying a new type of therapy or a new medication is trying a new outlook," I suggested.

"What do you mean? Do you think I have a bad attitude?"

"Your wish for relief and your intention to find help are natural and healthy. Where you could use an attitude adjustment is by taking more ownership of your condition and by having more patience with the process of healing."

"But I don't want this. I don't want to feel this way! I just want to feel better!"

"All of us who wish to help you want you to get better. Unfortunately, in the meantime you have a ton of anxiety. You own it. Even though you don't want it, it's yours. It's going to help a lot if you stop trying to run away from it and work on finding ways to manage it while we try to understand what caused it and find ways to resolve it."

To her credit, Lisa took this in. She did not fire me. She took some deep breaths, shook off some desperation, and began asking questions about how she could exercise more patience.

I suggested that, as soon as she notices she's feeling desperate, she should interrupt herself with a deliberate time-out and remind herself that her painful feelings and memories won't hurt her if she breathes through them and then talks about them with me and with others who care about her.

Patience can be hard won. It does not mean giving in to complacent suffering. It means being in the moment as much as possible, even when it's a lousy or miserable moment.

Healing is not a race. It doesn't have a timetable. It can't be forced. It may take longer than you want. Practicing patience will help you stay in pace with your flow of healing. That way it will be less turbulent.

Faith

If perseverance is a big bowl of determination filled with patience and a generous topping of faith, then what is faith? And why is it so important?

Faith is the belief that by letting go of control and allowing nature to take its course, things will proceed as they are meant to. Faith does not require religion. It is not necessary for you to believe in God to have faith in healing. It only requires that you believe there is a powerful force that results in repair and in growth. That healing works for you goes without saying. You could not have suffered all the bumps and scrapes and hurts in your life without noticing that things get better as a result of the persistent power of healing. Having faith in healing is realistic, and it helps healing do its job.

When you add faith to patience, you have good reason to stay in the present. When you add determination, you won't give up when the going gets tough. With perseverance, you will stay the course of your healing journey.

Gratitude

Gratitude helps the most when you have the least.

Try doing this every day: Spend three minutes having a gratitude ceremony. Everyone has their own way of giving thanks. Here's a suggestion:

Go someplace alone, preferably outside. Notice where you are.

Then notice more deeply. See, hear, smell, and feel the details of your location. Then begin your thanks.

Try giving thanks for life. You didn't ask for it. It was given to you. When you give thanks, you become more aware of its texture—what it's like to be alive even when it's a sad or scary or painful time. You are alive having an experience. You are alive with options.

Try giving thanks for the air you breathe, the water you drink, the food you eat, and the love you share. Try giving thanks for the shelter you have. Try giving thanks for the people who have shown you kindness. When times are hard, giving thanks for healing will help it to happen. Try giving thanks for this life even if you're not happy with it. Then stay quiet, breathe, and notice where you are.

Giving gratitude in this way will help to settle your restlessness. It will help to bring you into the moment.

It can be helpful to do a specific gratitude inventory. You can make a list on paper or in your mind. You can start it with "At least I have . . ." You can end this with "food, shelter, and water" or at least the capacity to find it. You have people in your life, even if they are of limited usefulness. You have the gift of resourcefulness. You can try new things. You have your mind and the capacity to reason things through. You have possessions that give you comfort and meaning. You have your past. You have your future. You have now.

Gratitude will help your attitude. It will help you stay level and keep your wings on when there's plenty to complain about. Gratitude helps to give meaning and purpose to your struggles and to your comforts. It helps to put the extremes of pain and pleasure in perspective, and it enhances the experience of ordinary life.

Science of Gratitude

Gratitude has been the subject of scientific research. Drs. Robert Emmons and Michael McCullough found that regularly expressing appreciation improves health and well-being. When they had people keep gratitude journals, those participants were more likely to practice other healthy behaviors, such as getting sufficient sleep and regular exercise, and having a more positive outlook. Emmons also found that people who expressed gratitude received more emotional support from their friends and relatives.[4]

A review of twenty-six scientific studies of gratitude consistently demonstrated a positive correlation between gratitude and happiness.[5] The studies found that when people expressed gratitude they were more agreeable, less envious, less materialistic, and more generous, and felt a greater sense of well-being. One study showed a highly positive correlation between gratitude and these feeling states: satisfaction with life, vitality, subjective happiness, optimism, and hope. When the subjects in the study practiced gratitude, psychological tests showed they were less depressed and less anxious.[6] In another study, subjects were divided into two groups for two weeks. One group was asked to keep a daily "gratitude journal" in which they were asked to list five things for which they were grateful. The other group was asked to keep a daily "burdens journal" in which they were asked to list five things that annoyed them. The group that practiced gratitude had measurably improved well-being and fewer physical symptoms, exercised more, and had increased optimism.[7]

Science often confirms what we already believe to be true. In this case, there's scientific evidence confirming that practicing gratitude will improve your outlook and lower anxiety and depression.

Adding the daily practice of gratitude to perseverance and self-acceptance will do wonders for your outlook, and it will lower the amount of anxiety and sadness you feel. Having curiosity about yourself without judgment and reminding yourself of your strengths will deepen your appreciation of yourself. You are more likely to see yourself as a strong person who has endured hardship if you can forgive your weaknesses and celebrate your strengths. Maintaining an attitude of perseverance will carry you through your darkest hours so that you can enjoy more pleasant times. Having gratitude for the gifts you have will help ease your mind and give you hope for your future.

Lisa's Reluctant Gratitude

Lisa attended a seminar about gratitude. Her friend Rachel insisted they go together.

Rachel had just been betrayed by her boyfriend of five years. She found out from a mutual friend that he was seeing someone else. Although he denied it, the evidence was too convincing to Rachel. Her friend saw him making out with someone behind a tree in the park. Then in the bathroom she discovered underwear she knew wasn't hers. She was crushed and turned to Lisa for support.

Lisa's father had died two years before, and her mother was not doing well. Lisa's boyfriend yelled at her a lot. He wanted to have a threesome, and he was using a lot of cocaine.

"Why should I go learn about gratitude when my life is so shitty?" Lisa asked.

"Maybe it will help," Rachel said. "I'm feeling at the end of my rope, and I'm ready to try anything. Anyway, here you are. You're my friend. I'm grateful for that."

Maybe Rachel has a point, *Lisa thought. Why not give it a try?*

When the two women arrived at the seminar, about thirty people were already there. The leader said, "There's a good chance that many of you feel you have little to be grateful for. Otherwise you probably wouldn't be here."

Lisa was all ears.

The leader explained how important gratitude is when you feel like everything has gone wrong. Gratitude, he explained, often opens the door for more goodness to enter your life.

Lisa wasn't convinced.

Then the leader asked for examples of gratitude. People had interesting things to say, like, I don't have a toothache. . . . My friend called me. . . . I love my dog. . . . I have a roof over my head. . . . I have faith that I will find love again.

Lisa started thinking about some reasons she had for gratitude. "I have my health. . . . I'm here with my friend. . . . My dog loves me. . . . I'm able to make a living. . . . Sometimes I feel happy when I don't want to."

After practicing gratitude for a few minutes, Lisa began to feel more hopeful about her life. She grasped that a daily gratitude ritual might help her endure her sadness. She realized she could spend time with her friend. She began to believe she could become less anxious and depressed.

In gratitude, Lisa found hope.

The more you bring gratitude into your everyday life, the more you'll find reason to be alive and reason to believe that your life is better than you thought. The spiritual exercise of gratitude is most helpful when you have the least. It will help you believe your life is worth living and you are worth healing.

Attitude Adjustment

Self-Acceptance
Celebrate your uniqueness.
Eliminate shame with curiosity.
Think of three positive attributes every time you
have a negative self-thought.
The longest relationship you'll have is with yourself;
make it a good one.

Perseverance
*(A big bowl of determination filled with patience
with a generous topping of faith)*
Never give up.
Apply determination to your patience.
Have faith that healing will strengthen you.
Keep going even when you don't want to.

Gratitude
Make a list of what you have and think about it.
Perform a daily three-minute gratitude ceremony.
Gratitude brings grace to perseverance and
strengthens self-acceptance.

CHAPTER 5

Behavior Change

Mindfulness, Exercise, Diet, and
Stress Management (MEDS)

*T*hese "MEDS" may be your most important prescription.
You'll heal your anxiety and depression faster and more effectively if you can make a few simple and gratifying changes in your behavior. These healing-enhancing behaviors will improve your mood, and because they promote wellness, they will improve your overall health—and they may even extend your life span. Adopting these behaviors may be all you'll need to resolve your anxiety or depression, and if they're not enough, they'll make anything you add, like therapy or medicine, work much better.

I recommend four behaviors that are especially helpful for anxiety and depression. I've seen them make a huge difference in my patients' recoveries, and I'll present scientific studies that confirm their effectiveness in reducing the symptoms of anxiety and depression.

The first letters of the behaviors I've chosen spell MEDS. I'm convinced these are the best MEDS you'll ever take:

Mindfulness

Exercise

Diet

Stress Management

When I recommend these behaviors to my patients, often I write them on a prescription pad. You'll see a sample MEDS prescription at the end of this chapter. It's a prescription you can write for yourself.

Despite the importance of adopting and sustaining healthy behaviors, few people actually manage to maintain them. Consider, for example, the many discarded diets and unused or hardly used health club memberships. Why is it so difficult for many people to sustain healthy behaviors? Most people don't like to do something that feels uncomfortable and doesn't give immediate gratification. Although these MEDS require some attention and effort, I'll show you how to incorporate them into your lifestyle with minimal disruption. The benefits you'll experience in your mood and in your overall wellness are well worth the small investment of time and energy needed to make these healing-enhancing behaviors part of your routine. I have seen people gain remarkable energy, strength, resilience, and relief of distress simply by spending a few minutes each day practicing these behaviors. Some of the people I've known who have adopted these behaviors have been able to stop taking their antianxiety and antidepressant pharmaceuticals, and those who do continue to take medicine have a better outcome when they practice these healthy behaviors at the same time.

Mindfulness

When you slow down and notice where you are, what you are doing, and how you feel, you are practicing mindfulness. Being in the moment aligns you with your reality. When you experience the fullness of the moment, you still your mind and reduce the turmoil you may be feeling.

Psychologists, psychiatrists, and neurophysiologists (scientists who study brain function) have researched the benefits of mindfulness. A study of mindfulness meditation showed it works better than medication for relief of anxiety.[8] Furthermore, the researchers showed that meditation lacked the side effects of pharmaceuticals, and it produced long-lasting benefits for the brain.

Other types of mindfulness practice have been found effective for clinical anxiety in controlled trials. The same study compared mindfulness-based stress reduction (MBSR) to stress management education. When MBSR included meditation and yoga, it was found to be superior to stress management education alone. In fact, MBSR resulted in greater resilience and self-esteem and is considered by the study's authors to be a reasonable option to treatment with medication.

Mindfulness Meditation

Mindfulness meditation has been studied in the laboratory.[9] A single eight-hour day of meditation practice was actually shown to alter the genetic expression of inflammation. Compared to the start of the day, there was a measurable decrease in circulating inflammatory markers by the end of a day of meditating. Some forms of depression and anxiety are known to involve inflammatory activity, which can be reduced by certain anti-inflammatory medications. This study showed that meditation had a similar effect.

You don't need to spend an entire day meditating to gain a significant benefit from meditation. Researchers studied a group of people who were highly stressed by giving care to family members who had dementia.[10] The caregivers were taught Kirtan Kriya meditation and instructed to meditate twelve minutes daily. At the end of eight weeks, the group of meditators had measurably affected sixty-eight genes involved in inflammation. The researchers concluded that the meditating subjects had less anxiety because they activated their anti-inflammatory genes and reduced their inflammation-producing genes, while the subjects reported feeling better able to deal with their stress.

Small periods of meditation and other mindfulness practices sprinkled throughout the day can lead to measurable changes in the brain. Richard Davidson, a neuroscientist who has studied for years how meditation changes the brain, has shown that short periods of meditation can change how you think, change how your brain works, and improve your overall well-being.[11]

Basic Shamatha Meditation

Basic mindfulness or concentration meditation is widely practiced and is well known for its calming effect. I recommend that you include it in your daily routine. By stilling your mind, even for a few minutes, you'll give your brain a rest and train it to be less anxious. You can accomplish this simply by focusing your thought on a single object of attention. For this lesson, I recommend focusing on your breath.

First, place yourself in a comfortable position. If you can, sit cross-legged with your hands on your knees. It's also okay to sit on a chair. Either way, keep your back and spine as straight as you comfortably can. Now become aware of your breathing. Since breathing happens automatically, you don't have to control it; you can simply observe it. Notice how it moves in and out of your body. Notice only that.

You'll begin to be distracted by twinges of physical discomfort. Ignore them. Bring your attention back to your breathing. Next, your mind will start to wander. You'll have thoughts about what you've done, what you plan to do next, what you're not doing, and what you think you should be doing instead of meditating. Ignore them—and bring your attention back to your breathing.

By doing this, you are training your mind to be still. According to the scientific studies I've cited, meditating this way has an effect on your brain and even your genes. Your circuits are being rerouted, and unhealthy inflammatory processes are reduced. This results in greater relaxation and lower anxiety. Meditating a few minutes each day teaches your mind to be still and less easily shaken. Repetitive meditation practice will lead to substantial gain in emotional stability and resilience. I recommend you practice it daily for at least three minutes when you wake up or when you go to bed. I also recommend you meditate when you feel fearful, rattled, or frustrated. Three minutes of meditation works better than a sedative, and it will leave you feeling more refreshed.

Sixty-Second Mindfulness Check-In

When you don't have time to meditate but your life feels like it's moving too fast, try taking a minute to connect with yourself by taking a *mindfulness check-in*.

1. Stop what you're doing.
2. Take a deep breath and then breathe normally.

3. With every sensation, notice what's happening around you.
4. Tune in to what's happening within you: What are you feeling in this moment?
5. Allow the feeling to exist without judging it.
6. Take a deep breath.
7. Reenter your busy life gently.

By taking a sixty-second mindfulness check-in, you'll interrupt your mad dash to accomplish too much in not enough time.

Exercise

Many people have told me that exercise is the best thing they can do for themselves. It relieves their aches and pains, lowers their blood pressure and blood sugar levels, and eases their minds. Once they start exercising and manage to establish a routine, they don't want to stop. That's what I hope for you.

You already know that exercise makes your muscles stronger. It will give you greater endurance, stronger bones, and better sleep. Did you know that it will also strengthen your brain?

Regular exercise has been shown to increase the size of your brain's hippocampus, a part of your brain that has a lot to do with memory and emotions. The hippocampus tends to shrink in late adulthood, which increases your risk for dementia. Exercise training has been shown to increase the size of your hippocampus and improve memory function.[12]

Exercise has also been shown to increase the amount of brain-derived neurotrophic factor (BDNF) in your brain. BDNF is essential for good brain health. It stimulates the formation of new brain cells, increases your brain's capacity to absorb new information, and improves neuroplasticity, the capacity of your brain to handle stress.[13]

My patients tell me that they feel on top of their game when they exercise regularly. It's more than a metaphor. When you strengthen your body, you'll likely have more energy, sleep better, look better, have better sex, and pay closer attention to your diet and your health. When your body is stronger, you'll be able to do more with it, and you'll be able to handle more stress. You'll be less likely to avoid necessary or important tasks and more likely to rally when needed. When the chips are down and it feels like life is throwing too much at you, a workout can do wonders. It can convince you that you are strong and that you are able to persist and prevail. But how can you manage to exercise when you don't feel like it?

You may need to adjust your outlook about exercise. You may be thinking exercise is too hard, but it doesn't need to be. You may think exercise will be too uncomfortable or even painful; you may think exercise is too inconvenient or that you won't look good enough or you won't do it the right way. You may expect too much of yourself. There's a way around that: Do less exercise.

Your Three-Minute Workout

With exercise, a little goes a long way if you do it consistently. For years I've been recommending a daily three-minute workout, and many of my patients and friends have benefited from making it part of their daily routine. When they make a three-minute daily workout a nonnegotiable requirement, it creates a strong base for whatever else they may choose to do. If they don't do any other exercise, at least they keep themselves in good condition with their nonnegotiable three-minute workout.

People think I am kidding when I tell them not to change into workout clothing because it will slow them down. I explain to them that their workout will be over by the time they change their shoes. I tell people not to go to the gym unless they want to, but be sure to include their three-minute workout with whatever else they do at the gym.

If you decide to do a daily three-minute workout, your workout should be nonnegotiable. You must do it sometime during your day— maybe when you wake up or before lunch or between meetings or before a regular activity. Make your workout more important than anything except a life-threatening situation.

Think of your workout as medicine that will keep you in good health with a clear mind. Don't take a pill when you feel troubled; have a three-minute workout. Don't have a drink or a donut; have a set of push-ups or squats.

Start with stretching. For at least thirty seconds, stretch all your body parts that work—but not enough to cause pain. Stretching helps protect you from muscle and joint injuries during your workout.

Your three-minute exercise routine should be tailored to your needs and desires. If you have an arthritic condition, exercise so that you maintain flexibility without causing injury. If you have a heart condition, don't start with a high-intensity burst. Check with your doctor, and if you have any question or doubt, ask what type or degree of exercise would be safe for you.

If you're generally healthy and in reasonably good shape, begin your routine with a set of push-ups, a set of abdominal crunches, and a set of squats. This will improve your core strength and give you a full body tone-up. If you prefer, walk or trot up and down a set of stairs a few times, or run in place for a few minutes. If you attract attention, invite your spectators to join you. If you sweat, don't worry about it. It's not the kind of sweat that stinks.

If you can't walk, raise yourself up in your seat with your arms or lift something moderately heavy. Moving quickly and safely in a self-propelled wheelchair is a great workout.

Make sure your workout is brief—about as long as a trip to the bathroom—and exertional. Exertional means you can't have a conversation because you are focused on your workout and breathing too hard to talk. Don't make your workout so hard that you won't want to keep doing it. The point is to find a quick toning workout that you'll want to do because it helps you feel stronger and more confident. In other words, make your workout sustainable. If you don't feel like doing your workout, do it anyway, but cut it in half. Do five push-ups on your knees instead of ten with your toes. Do ten squats instead of twenty. Walk up three flights of stairs instead of six. You'll do more another time if you don't burn yourself out by forcing or overdoing your workout. Just be sure to do *something*; you'll feel better if you do half your workout than if you don't work out at all. Push yourself enough so that you'll feel accomplished.

After you work out, notice your improved muscle tone, your deep breathing, and your heart rate. Visualize how you are strengthening your bones and muscles and sharpening your mind. Visualize how you feel stronger and look better, and how you can do more.

The benefits of a brief intense workout were reported by Dr. Izuni Tabata and the National Institute of Fitness and Sports in Tokyo. Dr. Tabata and his team compared the effects of brief exercise sessions to longer ones.[14] They had a group of people do moderate-intensity exercise for an hour. (Moderate intensity means it's possible but difficult to have a conversation during exercise.) The other group did high-intensity interval training (conversation not possible) in eight cycles of twenty seconds of maximum effort followed by ten seconds of rest for a total of four minutes and twenty seconds. The moderate-exercise group worked out five days a week for six weeks, and the high-intensity group worked out four days a week for six weeks. Clearly (and surprisingly), a brief high-intensity workout had a better outcome than one hour of moderate exercise. At the end of the six-week study, the one-hour group had increased their aerobic fitness but not their muscle strength or size. The four-minute-and-twenty-second group did just as well with their aerobic fitness, but their anaerobic (muscle) fitness improved by 28 percent.[15]

The data confirm what I've experienced as well as the feedback I've received from friends and patients. People feel stronger and fitter with very little time commitment. In fact, there's such a small time requirement that there's plenty of time left in the day to go to Pilates or yoga classes, or to play tennis or swim. Doing your daily three-minute workout increases the likelihood that you'll enjoy your favorite sport, and you'll be less likely to injure yourself while you do it.

Importance of Exercise for Your Mind

Exercise is so important for your mind that it has become part of the recommended practice guidelines of the American Psychiatric Association. Exercise has been formally recognized as an "intervention option" in the treatment of major depressive disorder since November 2010. In a clinical trial, exercise was "prescribed" in "low doses" (40 to 60 minutes per week) for one group and "high doses" (150 minutes per week) to people suffering from depression who experienced no benefit from medication.[16] Those in the group who were prescribed higher doses of exercise received a greater benefit.

Researchers found that exercise also had a positive effect on the subjects' epigenetics. There was a reduction in blood levels of pro-inflammatory cytokines, which are elevated in some people with depression.

In another study, nearly 34,000 nondepressed Norwegian adults were followed over eleven years. The researchers showed that those subjects who exercised at least one hour weekly experienced 12 percent fewer cases of depression than the subjects who did not exercise at least one hour weekly.[17]

Whether you decide on a 150- or a 21-minute-per-week exercise routine, plenty of evidence shows that you'll feel better and that your efforts will help prevent or reduce the severity of depression.

Exercise, Anxiety, and Panic Disorder

With aerobic activity, levels of endorphins and enkephalins are boosted, and stress-producing cortisol levels are reduced. You'll feel better physically and emotionally. Over time, exercise is associated with greater satisfaction with life. In a large study in the *International Journal of Psychiatry in Medicine*, exercise was declared to be "an effective and cost-efficient treatment alternative for a variety of anxiety disorders."[18]

In addition to having benefits for chronic or intermittent anxiety, exercise has been found to help panic attacks and panic disorder.

If you've never had a panic attack, I hope you never will. During a panic attack, you feel like you're about to die or be attacked. In addition to complete and utter terror, your heart races, your breathing becomes so strained that you feel like you are suffocating, and you become filled with a desperate need to escape your situation. You might even go to an emergency room to find out if you're having a heart attack.

Panic attacks can happen to anyone, and having a panic attack does not necessarily mean you'll start having more panic attacks. During times of intense overwhelm or fear of danger, it's not unusual to have a panic attack.

Having the ongoing condition of panic disorder is a different matter. Some people with true panic disorder have persistently repeating panic attacks, as many as six or more in one day. Panic disorder is a hardwired genetic condition for some people. Psychotherapy can help, and sometimes medication is needed.

In a very convincing landmark study, exercise was compared to a medication known to help panic disorder (clomipramine) and to a placebo. Over the course of ten weeks, forty-six people with known panic disorder were divided into three groups and "treated" with aerobic exercise, clomipramine, or a placebo. The exercise group did so well that the authors concluded that exercise alone would be a valuable treatment of panic disorder for people who are unwilling or unable to take medication. It's significant that a healing enhancer—exercise—could be classified as a form of treatment for panic disorder (as well as for depression) by prestigious medical journals.[19] It's significant also that something that can be so good for your body can help to ease your mind.

Lisa's Insult-Driven Workout

Lisa's motivation to work out happened in a surf shop. While Lisa was growing up on Long Island, one of her escapes from her father's drinking and raging was to go surfing. Because her father was successful with his three hardware stores, Lisa's family could afford to live in a comfortable home on the water on the North

Shore of Long Island. They had a dock and a boat.

Lisa was a strong and confident swimmer and was on swim teams as a child. Because she had an edge and a need to escape, she was drawn to surfing on the South Shore of Long Island. She especially loved it when there was a storm off shore and the waves were high. With a wetsuit, she could surf year-round. In fact, it was better in the winter—bigger waves and smaller crowds.

When she started surfing, however, despite her expertise as a swimmer, Lisa had trouble getting out past the waves in order to surf them in.

Where she surfed, it was often necessary to paddle directly into the waves because of the way they were breaking. Sometimes it was necessary to "turn turtle" when a big wave was about to hit. That meant flipping the board over and holding on underneath. The wave would sweep over the board while her body acted like a sea anchor, slowing her down so that she wasn't pushed too far back to shore. Paddling out through big waves was very tiring and required strength and breath-holding skills.

Lisa kept getting pushed back to shore. She felt like giving up. She went to the surf shop where she bought her board to ask what she was doing wrong.

"You're too weak!" the owner said. "That's what's wrong."

That made Lisa angry. "I'm not weak! I was on a swim team. I can pick up my older brother!"

The owner said, "You're weak. If you were stronger you could make it through the break."

Lisa was shocked and insulted. She was about to walk out, but she noticed that several people were listening to her conversation and were waiting to hear what she would say.

"Okay, let's say I'm too weak. What should I do?"

The owner didn't miss a beat. "Push-ups! Every day. Start low, go slow, and build up gradually. Here, I'll show you."

He got on the floor and did a set of fifty push-ups. Then he shifted to his back and did a set of thirty crunches. He rolled on the carpet as he touched his elbows to his opposite knees. Then he stood up and did a set of squats. He lowered himself by bending his legs as if to sit on a chair and then stood back up. "It wouldn't hurt to do a few pull-ups," he said, breathing heavily. He had a pull-up bar in the doorway to his office, where he did a set of ten.

Lisa got it. She absorbed the insult and grabbed the challenge. She knew he meant well.

Eventually Lisa could do seventy push-ups, followed by fifty crunches and sixty squats. She got stronger. When she was near the pull-up bar she put in the doorway to her bedroom, she would do ten. Some days she would do less and some days more. She tried to be reasonable about it. If her energy was low, she would do half as many as when she felt on top of her game.

She would do a set of push-ups just before her shower or just before lunch or dinner. When she thought about not doing her workout, she thought about the surf-shop owner. She pictured his face and the people staring at her.

Lisa never changed her clothes to do a set of exercises. One set took less than five minutes. When she visited friends, she did a set in their bathroom. They never suspected she was doing her daily workout. It took as long as taking a leisurely trip to the toilet or putting on makeup.

Lisa required herself to do at least one set every day. Often she would do more than one set. Her reward was how she felt and *how she looked. She stopped having back pain, and she had more energy. Because she felt stronger physically, she felt more confident and capable. She could also paddle out through the breaks, catch a good wave, and ride it back to shore.*

The Three-Minute Workout

Do something strenuous at least once daily. Don't change your clothing; it will take too long and distract you, and exercise sweat doesn't stink enough to worry about it.

- Walk or run up and down a set of stairs (carefully).
- Do a set of push-ups followed by crunches, squats, and toe rises.
- Walk briskly around the block or spend a few minutes on a piece of exercise equipment.

Also, link exercise to an activity.

- Before a meal
- Before a meeting
- As soon as you get home from work

Go to the gym or do other exercise for fun, but make your daily three-minute workout a requirement. It will clear your head and make you healthier, and you may even live longer because of it.

Diet

Food can be medicine that tastes good, and as with pharmaceuticals and supplements, food should be chosen and dosed properly. The food in your diet should also be chosen according to your personal needs and preferences. Because everyone is different, a diet that promotes healing for one person may not suit another. How do you decide what's the best diet for your mind and your body?

Until we have complete genetic dietary profiling, we only have a few crude tests. We also have trial and error. But don't trust only your gut on decisions about food. It could get hijacked along with your brain by unhealthy food cravings.

When you consider the diet that will be healthiest for you and will best reduce anxiety and depression, you'll be facing a dizzying array of choices. Here are some often competing suggestions for diets to help reduce anxiety and depression that I've gleaned from a variety of writings in popular literature.

- Eat like a caveman: meat and a few vegetables.
- Eat only plants.
- Avoid all grains.
- Avoid fats.
- Eat fats.
- Eat like an old Mediterranean.
- Eat like a Japanese fisherman.
- Eat foods that are good for your weak chakras.
- Eat foods that match your astrological sign.

There seem to be as many diets as there are opinions about what's healthy. My recommendations for diets that can help reduce anxiety and relieve depression are based on a survey of the current scientific literature. Although the literature has its flaws and biases, it can give some helpful information.

Fortunately, what's good for your mind appears to be good for your body. If a diet promotes healing for your mind, it's likely to do so for the rest of you. My wish for you is that you live as long as possible and in the best health possible. The diets I recommend for anxiety and depression can help your body as well as your mind.

Healthy Eating Promotes Healing

When your diet is in alignment with the needs of your body and mind, healing flows evenly and effectively. When you eat food that is bad for you, healing becomes disjointed, disharmonious, and derailed. Your flow of healing needs a safe and healthy diet to stay on track.

Starting with safety, one food in particular is not safe for you and can worsen your anxiety and depression: sugar. Nutritionists and medical experts agree with this statement: Sugar is bad for you.

Sugar is bad for your mind and it's bad for your body. It can be as addictive as nicotine. Like nicotine, sugar causes serious health problems, and it can mess with your mind.

Most people agree that sugar is largely responsible for the obesity epidemic as well as astonishingly high rates of diabetes, metabolic syndrome, heart disease, and premature mortality.

Fluctuations in blood glucose result from eating sugar-laden food, which causes energy and mood changes. When you consume sugar, your mood and energy are immediately elevated. Assuming you manufacture effective levels of insulin, your insulin response to a sugar load will cause your blood sugar to plummet, leaving you tired, depressed, and anxious. If you have insulin resistance, which places you at risk of diabetes, your body and mind develop tolerance to chronically elevated blood glucose levels. This can make you feel tired and depressed, as well as suffer metabolic illnesses (high blood pressure, diabetes, and coronary artery disease). Your concentration can become impaired and your quality and quantity of life can be reduced.

Even if you don't have diabetes or a genetic predisposition to it, you could develop it if you keep eating sugar. If you have a healthy insulin response, the fluctuations in mood and energy are not doing you any favors. No matter how much willpower you think you have, sugar makes you want more sugar.

There's a simple answer to this problem. For the sake of your mind, your body, and your life, stop eating sugar.

Try a sugar detox. No sugar for thirty days. See what happens. You may have trouble concentrating at first as your brain realigns itself. You may go into mourning. You're likely to have some craving. Resist your craving for sugar; don't give into it. You'll soon feel lighter and more energetic. Your mood and energy will become steadier, and your concentration will improve. You'll feel better, and you'll live longer.

Sugar by Any Other Name . . .

Don't be fooled by the labels you read. Sugar is present in food in many forms, including sucrose (table sugar), high fructose corn syrup, lactose, maltose, honey, agave, molasses, and rice syrup. Foods with synthetic sweeteners like sucralose, saccharin, and aspartame can keep your craving for sweets active even though they don't contain sugar. Artificial sweeteners can cause you to return to sugar.

Eliminating sugar is a great first step for helping to establish a steady mood, steady energy, and improved concentration.

Next Step: Reduce Your Glycemic Index

The glycemic index (GI) is a measurement of how much a carbohydrate-containing food raises your blood glucose (blood sugar) level. The higher GI a food has, the more it will raise your blood sugar. Some foods have such a high GI that they rival table sugar in their effect on your blood sugar level.

The American Diabetes Association has a list of low-, medium-, and high-GI foods. Based on a GI of 100 for pure sugar (glucose), foods with a high GI have a GI of 70 or more.

Eating a high-GI food can be the same as eating a candy bar. The same fluctuations in mood and energy along with impairment of concentration can occur.

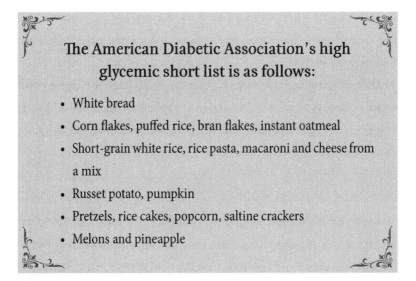

The American Diabetic Association's high glycemic short list is as follows:

- White bread
- Corn flakes, puffed rice, bran flakes, instant oatmeal
- Short-grain white rice, rice pasta, macaroni and cheese from a mix
- Russet potato, pumpkin
- Pretzels, rice cakes, popcorn, saltine crackers
- Melons and pineapple

The glycemic index of a food is lowered by its fiber content. Eating whole fruit is better than drinking fruit juice. Without the fiber, drinking fruit juice is like drinking sugar-filled soda.

If you intend to help your mind and your body by eliminating sugar, do the same with high-glycemic foods. That way you'll have less craving for carbs, and your mood, energy, and concentration will improve.

Benefits of an Anti-Inflammatory Diet

Some of the information about anti-inflammatory diets comes from the studies of celiac disease (CD) and gluten sensitivity (GS). Both CD and GS involve an allergic response to gluten. Symptoms of CD and GS can include gastrointestinal as well as psychological distress. Celiac disease, also called sprue, is an inflammation of the small intestine caused by a gluten allergy. Many of the people who suffer from CD also suffer depression and anxiety. Researchers have discovered that when sufferers of celiac disease and gluten sensitivity follow a strict gluten-free diet, their symptoms of depression and anxiety usually improve.[20]

Even if you don't have celiac disease or gluten sensitivity, your anxiety or depression could be worsened by gluten. In his book *Grain Brain*, neurologist and nutritionist David Perlmutter writes, "It is [my] belief that gluten is a modern poison." He shows convincingly that "Inflammation . . . is the cornerstone of many brain disorders," and advises a gluten-free diet to prevent damage to the brain.[21]

I recommend that my patients try a gluten-free diet if they have depression or anxiety along with an autoimmune or other inflammatory condition. This recommendation is supported by the finding that antidepressants have anti-inflammatory effects because they reduce inflammatory chemicals in the brain called cytokines, and they enhance the release of anti-inflammatory agents in the brain.[22] After a few weeks of a gluten-free diet some of my patients report less depression, less anxiety, less obsessional rumination, and better concentration. In some cases, they have fewer aches and pains and a general feeling of well-being.

Developing an anti-inflammatory lifestyle with regular exercise and meditation along with a no-sugar, low-glycemic, gluten-free diet may be a good idea for everyone. It's certainly a good idea if you are depressed and have inflammatory conditions like arthritis or fibromyalgia, or if you have an auto-immune disorder like psoriasis or lupus.

I recommend you avoid sugar and high-glycemic food no matter what type of diet you adopt. One of the most popular diets for good health and good mood is the Mediterranean diet, which many people consider healthy, delicious, and easy to follow.

The Mediterranean Diet

The health benefits of the Mediterranean diet have been studied extensively. A Spanish study, the PREDIMED (Prevencion con Dieta Mediterranea [Prevention with Mediterranean diet]) followed 7,500 people ages fifty-five to eighty.[23] One-third of the study group simply reduced fat in their diet. One-third ate a Mediterranean diet supplemented with nuts. The final third followed a Mediterranean diet supplemented with extra virgin olive oil. Within five years, the two groups using the Mediterranean diet were 30 percent less likely to suffer a heart attack or stroke or to die from heart-related causes.[24]

The Mediterranean diet they used relied heavily on fresh fruits and vegetables along with legumes, such as kidney beans, garbanzo beans, and lentils. It included moderate portions of unrefined and whole-grain bread and pasta. Moderate amounts of yogurt and cheese were included. Fish was the main protein source, along with three or four eggs per week. Chicken was allowed, and red meat intake was restricted to one or two portions per week with no processed meats. A moderate amount of alcohol was included for those non-alcoholics whose religion would allow it. Men had no more than two drinks per day (two six-ounce glasses of wine) and women no more than one. Red wine was the alcoholic beverage studied. Do not include alcohol in your diet if you have or if you have had a drinking problem.

To be avoided in the study were sugar-sweetened beverages, including fruit juices. (Fresh fruit with its natural fiber is medium to low glycemic, but fruit juice is high glycemic—nearly as high as sugary sodas.) Also avoided were desserts, baked goods, and anything high in refined carbohydrates.

One group supplemented the Mediterranean diet with extra nuts. They consumed 30 grams per day of mixed nuts: 15 grams of walnuts, 7.5 grams of hazelnuts, and 7.5 grams of almonds.

The surprising finding was that the group who added nuts to their Mediterranean diet had a 25 percent reduced incidence of depression. Investigators looked at a subgroup of people who had adult-onset (type 2) diabetes and included walnuts in their diet; they had a 41 percent reduction of depression compared to the people who did not include any nuts in their diet.[25]

How could nuts, especially walnuts, have such a strong depression-preventing effect in everyone, but especially for those with adult-onset diabetes? Could it be that something in the nuts (especially the walnuts) works especially well for a genotype or epigenotype that includes susceptibility to diabetes? Could a particular substance have an antidepressant or protective effect for that particular genetic subgroup?

Whether they include nuts in their diet or not, many people feel the Mediterranean diet is a reasonable compromise between the usual carbohydrate- and processed-food-laden diet and a more austere low-glycemic and gluten-free diet. For some, the Mediterranean diet provides the optimal balance of nutrients to promote healing for the mind. For those who are adversely affected by gluten, the Mediterranean diet is an insufficient compromise. The gluten in pasta and the high-glycemic index of wine can fuel carbohydrate craving and brain inflammation. For some, a strict gluten-free and low-glycemic-index diet is necessary.

Educate yourself about dietary options. Until we can tell you more about your genetic makeup and what best influences it, you may have to experiment. If you try a new diet, give yourself a month or two on it if you can. Just as with other healing enhancements, it can take that long to tell if something you've tried is working for you.

Omega-3 Fatty Acids and Mood

We've known since researcher Andrew Stoll reported it in 1999 that omega-3 fatty acids can help stabilize the mood fluctuations of bipolar disorder.[26] Omega-3 fatty acid in the form of EPA (eicosapentaenoic acid) was also found to be helpful for depression. In fact, in one study, sixty depressed people were given either an antidepressant (Prozac) or extra omega-3 fatty acid. The group receiving extra omega 3 did just as well as the group receiving an antidepressant.[27] Those results have been replicated in other studies.

Although most of these studies involved the addition of concentrated omega-3 fatty acids, studies have also been conducted on the effect of fish consumption on mood. Since fish contains high levels of omega-3 fatty acids, comparisons have been made between people who regularly eat fish and those who don't. In one large study, fish consumption was especially helpful for men who suffered severely depressed mood.[28] In another extensive analysis of multiple studies, greater seafood consumption was clearly linked to lower rates of depression and bipolar disorder.[29] Conversely, not eating fish or eating fish very infrequently was linked to higher rates of depression and bipolar disorder.

A very large study from 1998 showed that the amount of fish consumption by country correlated highly with the frequency of depression in that country.[30] Japan had the lowest rate of depression. It also had the highest annual consumption of fish (140 pounds per person).

If you decide to boost your omega-3 fatty acid level with fish, be careful about how much mercury you get. Mercury is a toxin that concentrates in fish that are higher on the food chain (fish that eat other fish). Fish with the highest mercury levels are swordfish, shark, halibut, tuna, bluefish, and bass. Lower levels can be found in cod, flounder, haddock, and salmon. Mercury is toxic to the central nervous system and can cause impaired vision, hearing, and speech, and also muscle weakness. Pregnant women should be especially careful and limit their exposure to mercury as much as possible.

What If You're Vegetarian or Vegan?

Reports are conflicting about the effects of a vegetarian diet on anxiety and depression. A German study comparing vegetarians to nonvegetarians found higher rates of anxiety and depression for the vegetarians. However, the study could not conclude that following a vegetarian diet caused anxiety or depression because most of the vegetarians were depressed or anxious before they switched to a vegetarian diet.[31] In another study comparing sixty vegetarians to sixty-eight nonvegetarians, the vegetarians had significantly better mood scores than the nonvegetarians.[32]

Most vegetarian diets include alpha linoleic acid (ALA), a type of omega-3 fatty acid found in flaxseed, walnut, and soy (including tofu). Some vegetarians and vegans increase their intake of these foods in order to increase their omega-3 fatty acid levels. Aside from the apparent antidepressant benefit of walnuts previously cited in the Mediterranean diet study, there's no clear evidence that increasing ALA intake improves mood.[33] Based on the studies I've reviewed, I find no reason to recommend either stopping or starting a vegetarian diet for the sake of mood.

Probiotic Food for Your Mind

Did you know you are the host organism for nearly 40 trillion bacteria that live in your gut?[34] As long as the bacteria in your gut live in proper percentages with one another, your bacterial traveling companions will help keep your gastrointestinal tract functioning well, and they will even help keep you from becoming depressed. Your delicately balanced ecosystem of gut bacteria is called your *microbiome*, and researchers have found that a well-balanced microbiome contributes to a well-balanced mind.[35]

Imbalances in the microbiome have been linked with anxiety and depression,[36] and research suggests that microbiome imbalances causing emotional distress can be partially reversed with properly selected probiotics. Probiotics that help you have a more positive outlook are called *psychobiotics*. An eight-week randomized controlled trial comparing the probiotic *Bifidobacterium longum* to placebo showed that twice as many people who took the probiotic experienced significant reduction of depression and significant improved quality of life compared to those who took the placebo.[37] Brain imaging studies of those who felt better showed reduced limbic activity, suggesting that the probiotic in the gut improved activity in the brain—the work of a true psychobiotic.

One easy way to keep your microbiome balanced is by including fermented food in your diet, which adds probiotics to your gut. Probiotics are the good ("pro") bacteria that are healthy for your body and for your mind. Foods containing live probiotics include yogurt, sauerkraut, kombucha, kimchi, natto and tempeh (fermented soybeans), kefir, miso soup, sourdough bread, and soft aged cheese. Probiotic foods compete with the bad bacteria that are boosted by a diet high in sugar.

Some people prefer to take probiotics in capsule form. Many manufacturers offer live probiotic organisms in capsules. They are so tiny that billions can fit in a normal-sized capsule. This delivers a higher quantity of probiotics than you'll generally find in food. If you wish to try probiotics in capsule form, start with a low dose. Too much at once might destabilize your microbiome and cause you to have diarrhea.

More work is needed to determine which probiotics might help reduce anxiety and depression, but if you enjoy the taste of probiotic foods, they may help your mind heal.

So much research pointing to the effects of food on anxiety and depression confirms that following a healthy diet is a very important part of an effective healing plan for anxiety and depression. No matter what diet you follow, I recommend that you eliminate sugar and reduce your intake of high-glycemic foods. If you feel better without gluten, eliminate it from your diet. If you enjoy nuts and nut butters, they may help reduce depression. The same is true for omega-3 fatty acids and alpha linoleic acid–containing foods. Every time you reach for something to eat, think about whether it's likely to be good for your body and your mind.

Stress Management

Stress is inevitable. There's no avoiding it. In your busy life you must tolerate stress and difficult times. Sometimes you force yourself to do too much, and sometimes too much is asked of you. Sometimes emotions stirred up by a stressful interaction or event are overwhelming and unbearable.

The right amount of stress is a moving target between emptiness and overwhelm. What's the right amount of stress for you? When is it enough to keep things interesting, and when is it too much to bear? How do you keep yourself active, sharp, and creative without depleting yourself and making yourself sick?

Your Stress Threshold

You can only take so much. Too much stress will overrun your capacity to manage it. When you are over the top, you have exceeded your stress threshold. It's important to know where that threshold is so that you can avoid it or know what to do about it.

If you spend too much time above your stress threshold, you are likely to suffer symptoms of anxiety, panic, and even despair. If the stress lasts too long, you run the risk of having those symptoms develop into an anxiety or depressive illness. You also run the risk of developing a medical condition like ulcers, hypertension, diabetes, or chronic back pain.

You may not be able to handle as much stress as your friends or even your relatives. Although your genes influence your stress threshold level, so do childhood adversity, medical problems, age, and current life events. The more problems you have, the more likely that your threshold for stress is low and that you could exceed your stress threshold.

As you can see in the following illustration, your stress threshold can be exceeded multiple times in your life. If your threshold is naturally high, you'll be able to handle more stress before you exceed it. If your threshold is low, it won't take much stress to trigger a problem. The next time you feel overwhelmed and stressed, think about what caused it and what you might be able to do to reduce it. When you learn where your stress threshold is, you won't be so surprised when you exceed it and you may be able to take steps to stay below it.

Your Stress Threshold

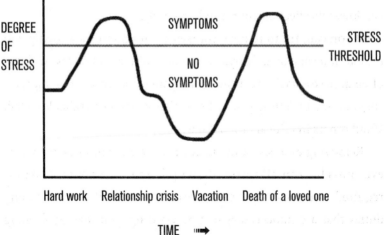

When you exceed your stress threshold, symptoms can develop. When you stay too long above your stress threshold, symptoms can become hardened into illnesses. When you stay below your stress threshold, symptoms are less likely to emerge.

R.I.P. Your Stress

Here's a simple acronym to help you manage your stress: R.I.P.: remove, improve, and pace. When you effectively manage your stress, you reduce its harmful effect on your mind and on your body. Keeping your stress level below your stress threshold is the goal. Removing harmful stress, improving the nature of your stress, and pacing yourself will help.

R: Remove Unhealthy Stress

Too much stress can lead to extreme distress and worsen physical illness. When stress is repetitive and unrelenting, it can turn on a condition that can be hard to turn off. Too much stress can activate the genes that switch on panic disorder, depression, or physical problems like acid reflux or low back pain. By removing unnecessary stress, you can lower its effect on your mind and body.

If you can, try to remove yourself from unnecessary gossip and drama. Interpersonal distress is a powerful form of stress, and it is often unnecessary. You can announce your resignation from interpersonal drama by letting people know that you're not available to talk about others in critical or hurtful ways.

Removing excessive and unnecessary work commitments wherever possible can also help. If you pile more on yourself than is required, you cause yourself unnecessary stress. If you are adding duties that are unnecessary or unrewarding, you may be keeping yourself from doing things for yourself that would be good for you.

No one knows how to take care of you better than you. Saying no when you need to and removing unnecessary stress are ways you can help yourself.

I: Improve Your Life

The quality of your activities has a big effect on the quality of your life. Engaging in activities that you find meaningful and fulfilling enhances your life. Even though they require energy from you, high-quality activities give it back. Meaningful and fulfilling actions bring satisfaction and reduce distress and stress.

If your work is not fulfilling or meaningful, is there some way you could help to make it so? Could the quality of your interactions at work be improved? Could you focus more on the parts of your job that seem important or meaningful? If there is no way to improve meaning and enjoyment in your work, could you balance it with fulfilling activities outside work? Would a volunteer activity or a hobby improve the quality of your life or provide a pleasant diversion? If something is important to you and you don't feel you have time for it, is there a way to make time for it or fit it into your schedule?

Improving the quality of and meaning in your life may involve improving the quality of your relationships. Perhaps some repair work on a current relationship would help. It might help make your life more meaningful to reach out and reconnect with someone who has been important to you. Maybe you need to bring more people into your life or spend less time with those people you find draining.

P: Pace Yourself

Pacing yourself involves external and internal regulation. It means dialing down the intensity inside and outside yourself. Let's first look at how you can dial down your schedule.

Scheduling too much in too little time may help you feel connected and distract you from inner emptiness, but it's bad for your body and bad for your mind. Slowing down may seem like a simple solution, but it is one too easily forgotten. Intentionally creating gaps in your schedule instead of desperately running to the next thing can lower your pulse and your anxiety.

Sleep. When you dial down your schedule, make sure you're scheduling enough time for sleep. Most adults need seven hours nightly.[38] Convincing yourself to go to bed when you want to stay up or to get up when you want to stay in bed can be difficult. Nighttime or early morning may be the only time you feel you have for yourself. That's okay as long as you schedule enough time to sleep. Your body, including your brain, needs to recover. Requiring yourself to get enough sleep may sound restricting, but it's worth it to help you manage your stress.

Spending. The principle of dialing down intensity can be applied to money. Our society encourages spending. Having nice things, going places, and doing fun things are wonderful, but when you spend more than you earn, you create unnecessary stress. Spending less than you earn reduces your stress and lightens your spirit. Just as important as pacing your schedule and sleep is pacing your spending.

Dial down internal stress. Pacing your inner intensity is as important as pacing the rate of your engagement with your world. If you can't dial down your external stress, at least you can dial down your inner intensity. It's not just the amount of work you do or how much you do for others that determines your degree of stress. Stress also results from the intensity or pressure you create within yourself.

You have more control than you realize when you are working or helping others too much. It may be difficult for you to tell when you are pushing yourself too hard, but it's the first thing you should consider when you're feeling pressured. The stress you put on yourself is the stress you can most easily reduce. Several variables can cause excessive intensity. They include placing more importance on an event or activity than it deserves, fear that you will disappoint others, worrying too much about what's going to happen next, and rushing when it's not required.

Some people can dial down their intensity directly, just by realizing and thinking about it. Others will assess their intensity pulse and take a few slow breaths or notice their surroundings in order to lower their internal pressure.

By dialing down your inner stress, you take control over the most important and the most manageable source of stress in your life: yourself.

R.I.P. Your Stress
(Remove, Improve, and Pace)

Remove sources of unnecessary stress:

- Gossip and drama
- Unnecessary activities
- Unfulfilling and draining relationships

Improve the quality of your stress:

- Find meaningful work with kind people
- Develop enjoyable hobbies and social connections
- Change your environment if it causes undue stress

Pace yourself to distribute your stress:

- Dial down your inner tension
- Take on less than you can manage
- Get enough sleep
- Spend less than you earn

Lisa's Threshold

"I am so stressed out!"

"What's wrong?" I asked.

"Everything! Everything is going wrong at once!"

"Like what?"

"I just lost two of my best employees. I was raided by a competitor who's been trying to steal my clients. He's a damn weasel who lies to my face. Now I'm going to have to call the clients on my A-list to try to get them back.

"Then my brother called. He invested half the money he inherited on a long-shot business that's going down the tubes. I think he's drinking too much. Then my ex–high school boyfriend Jake called to see what I've been up to. He's just ending a relationship, and I think he wants to go out. My computer system at work crashed, and I have expensive IT people up my butt! My friend Rachel wants to go to Aruba, and I don't think I can join her."

"Wow," I said. "That's a lot at once."

"You're telling me! This morning my washing machine started leaking, and I'm late for my period."

"Anything else?"

"I'm having gas pains, and I have no appetite. I started hyperventilating on my way to work. Fortunately, I knew it was a panic attack and talked myself down."

"Is there anything else you can do?"

"Who, me? You're the one with all the bright ideas. What do you think?"

"How about we take a look at what you're doing to take care of yourself?"

"*That's the last thing I can do right now. I have too much to do.*"

"*You're here,*" I pointed out.

"*That's true. I thought it would help to vent.*"

"*Definitely. Venting beats hyperventilating. It's important to talk through your sources of stress. But it's also important to manage your stress. I recommend you R.I.P. your stress.*"

"*What do you mean 'rip' it?*"

"*I mean 'R.I.P.': remove, improve, and pace. It means remove unnecessary stress, improve the quality of your time and effort, and pace yourself.*"

"*But there's nothing I can remove,*" Lisa said. "*I'm not doing enough as it is.*"

"*You can remove yourself from some of the drama,*" I said. "*If you simplify the messages you are giving your staff and stay out of the gossip, it will reduce your stress. Also, when you're feeling stressed and pressured, it's human nature to think about all the things you haven't done and start thinking you should do them now. Try to remove unnecessary projects from your list. You have enough going on as it is. The things you haven't done for a while and are not critical should be the first to go. Also, for now, it would help if you cut back your volunteer hours at the SPCA.*"

"*I don't know about that last thing. I get a lot of pleasure taking care of animals.*"

"*You've also said you want to take them all home. You don't need the added guilt just now. You might need to let your friends know that you'd like to get together with them some more.*"

"*What? I have no time as it is!*"

"*You've told me that the thing you find most relaxing, other than playing with your dog, Ginger, is having dinner with a friend.*

That's the 'I for Improve' part. If you can improve the quality of your time and your events, it will help reduce your distress."

"It would be nice to feel less alone with this pressure," Lisa said. "Maybe I'll give Rachel a call."

"Great idea," I said. "You can tell her you don't know yet if you'll be able to go with her to Aruba.

"Next there's 'P' for 'pacing.' As you're thinking and feeling about these crises, you're building up a head of steam inside. That pressure is what's causing your feelings of overwhelm and panic. If you can just slow down and breathe and realize that none of this is life-threatening, you might be able to sort it by importance and take it on bit by bit. You'll just get yourself more upset if you try to fix it all at once."

"Okay," Lisa said, nodding. "Remove unnecessary projects, pressures, and drama. Improve time spent with people. Pace my pressure and schedule. I think it's going to be harder than it sounds."

"Decompressing your busy life is worth the trouble. You'll have less heartburn and less heartache."

Bick Wanck, MD

www.bickwanckmd.com

MEDS

Mindfulness

3 minutes of meditation every evening.

Exercise

3 to 5 minutes of vigorous exercise daily (in whatever you
are wearing) before a meal or shower.

Diet

No sugar or low-refined grains.

High in fresh vegetables.

Consider adding probiotic foods.

Stress Management

Identify and stay below your stress threshold by dialing
down your inner and outer stress.

Get 7 hours of consolidated sleep.

Spend less than you earn.

CHAPTER 6

Compassionate Love

*Enjoy the various types of love
in your life, but cherish compassionate
love for its capacity to heal.*

W e are complex social creatures with simple needs: We need to love, and we need to feel loved. After all of the many generations of humans and various structures and organizations of human civilization, this fact remains abundantly clear: We need each other.

Even though we are our own worst enemies through warfare, crime, divorce, and abuse, we also care for each other and rely on each other. This is in our programming, our DNA. No matter how much of a mess we make of things, we still need love.

Science, literature, and art all demonstrate that love heals. It is the sublime and sweet elixir that gives meaning, purpose, and fulfillment to life. It soothes, nurtures, and helps us grow and repair. Love helps healing find its way.

You started out perfectly designed to be loved. As a baby, you were pure and innocent. You meant no harm to anyone. You needed to be cared for in order to survive. The way you looked, sounded, and smelled (hopefully) triggered an outpouring of love from those around you.

Your basic needs as an infant to be fed, cleaned, held, and protected continue for you as an adult. You still want to feel safe, cherished, and appreciated. You still need to feel that you are important to others—that you enrich their lives and they enrich yours.

Your capacity to love and to be loved may be your most important healing enhancer. By giving and receiving love, you create a home for healing. Knowing that you are not alone—that you are loved—gives you peace and comfort as your mind heals itself. Love creates a safe place for you to heal, and science has confirmed that compassionate love has a direct, positive effect on healing.

The Many Forms of Love

Love comes in many forms. Love can be exciting, dangerous, confusing, hurtful, comforting, or healing. The ancient Greeks described several types of love, and these descriptions remain relevant today.[39]

Eros is the passionate and intense love associated with sexual attraction and desire. It is an important part of romance, and it involves powerful interpersonal chemistry.

Philia is warm, friendly, companionable love. It is the love most commonly associated with strong friendship and strong feelings of association.

Storge is familial love. It is the love associated with forgiveness and tolerance. It involves commitment to a relationship and acceptance of the flaws of another person. *Storge* is the type of love a parent feels for a child or a sibling feels even though feelings have been hurt.

Pragma is logical love. It is part of realistically assessing people according to a list of pros and cons or level of desirability. It's also an important part of the process of "making do" with a relationship—deciding to stay despite its shortcomings.

Ludus is playful love. It's fun, flirtatious, and superficial. Sometimes it involves lying, cheating, and fickle behavior.

Mania is love out of control and often pursued out of need. It includes possessiveness and dependency and is characterized by insecurity.

Agape is selfless love. It is altruistic love characterized by giving and expecting nothing in return.

Compassionate love is sometimes called *altruistic love.* The term "compassionate love" was developed at a World Health Organization meeting about quality of life. Compassionate love is the type of love that most directly promotes healing. Loving and being loved with compassion involve genuine concern for the distress felt by another. Compassionate love is kind, respectful, and caring, and it's a very important part of an effective healing plan.

What Is Compassionate Love?

Compassionate love is kind and loving acceptance given to you by someone who is authentically present. When you are loved with compassion, all aspects of yourself are accepted with kindness.

You can give yourself compassionate love. When you accept yourself with kindness and compassion, your difficulties become easier to accept and manage.

Compassionate love creates a healing paradox: *Self-acceptance leads to change.* When you accept yourself with compassion, you more clearly see yourself and your situation. As your self-awareness increases, you become more aware of what you need. When you lovingly accept yourself with compassion, you are more likely to make choices that are good for you. Compassionate love helps you see what you need and gives you strength to take action.

The Science Behind Compassionate Love

Compassionate love has attracted the attention of social and biological scientists because of its importance to human well-being. It has been studied in society, the laboratory, and the classroom.

Compassionate love has received the attention of the Massachusetts Institute of Technology (MIT) and the World Health Organization (WHO). Millions of dollars of funding have gone into researching the characteristics and effects of compassionate love. *The Science of Compassionate Love: Theory, Research, and Applications* describes some of the outcomes of this work.[40] Compassionate love has also been described philosophically and theologically in *Altruism and Altruistic Love: Science, Philosophy, and Religion in Dialogue.*[41]

In a study of compassion meditation, researchers found that people who practiced meditation that includes wishing for the well-being of self, others, or the planet lowered interleukin-6, an inflammatory marker, and lowered serum and salivary cortisol levels (cortisol is a stress marker). The lowered cortisol levels indicated a reduction in physiologic stress, and the lower inflammation correlates with lower levels of anxiety and depression (see chapter 5). The subjects who practiced compassion meditation also lowered their distress scores. The researchers concluded that "engagement in compassion meditation may reduce stress-induced immune and behavioral responses."[42]

Along with reductions of inflammatory markers and stress hormones, other chemicals in your body change with giving and receiving compassionate love. Oxytocin, often referred to as the "cuddle hormone," rises during compassionate love just as it does when a parent loves a child. The same holds true for vasopressin, a chemical that rises in response to bonding experiences.

Sources of Compassionate Love

Even if you don't feel understood, even if you feel all alone, you have sources of compassionate love in your life if you open your heart to them. They may be a lover, friends, relatives, a pet, or a therapist. If you can find love in your heart for someone or something, you can find love in your heart for yourself. If you can find love for yourself, you will enhance your healing.

Love that enhances healing can help correct some of the harm that has come to you. Compassionate love validates your worthiness despite your self-doubt, and it provides relief from emptiness when you feel alienated and alone. Compassionate love opens doors to new perceptions, healthier perspectives, and brighter possibilities.

If things did not go well for you as a child, you may have trouble knowing whom to trust. This is one reason it is important to recognize the kind of love that heals so that you can safely allow it into your heart. Knowing what compassionate love looks like and knowing where to find it will help you choose the type of love that heals.

Since having compassionate love in your life is good for you, let's look at where to find it. Some of the sources may surprise you.

Compassionate Love of Self

Since your longest and most important relationship is with yourself, let's start with you.

Because you have times of suffering, just like everyone else in the world, you could do with some compassion toward yourself. If you practice showing compassion toward yourself, you'll learn how to show it to others. You also learn how to recognize it and accept it in return.

Compassionate love given to yourself is not selfish; it's self-fulfilling. It's not self-absorbed; it enhances your capacity to love and care for others. The better you can show loving-kindness and compassion to yourself, the better you can show it for those you meet. When you have compassion for yourself, you're more likely to have compassion for others.

Compassionate Love for and from Others

When you quiet your mind and reflect with affection and concern toward another person, it helps them, and it helps you. In the course of living, show compassion to the people who are most important to you. When you go home after a long, hard day, you probably want to relax and respond automatically and spontaneously to the people with whom you live. For the sake of healing, the opposite should be practiced. When you are with those who are most important in your life, you should be intentional and mindful and actively practice compassionate love. Your home life is likely to be more rewarding if you do.

People let their hair down and react poorly when they are tired and spontaneous. Compassionate love is not unconditional love. It requires kind intention. If you hurt or offend others, you cannot realistically expect them to love you with compassion unless you apologize or explain your behavior. Intentional compassion should be practiced with your greatest vigor when you are with those you love. If you truly care about them, and if you wish them to feel the same for you, they— and you—deserve the effort. Raising the bar to make sure you show compassion for those you love will raise the level of love in your life.

Those who express compassionate love to you are precious and important. Those people might include your lover, members of your family, friends, and others who care. But there are two others you may not have considered sources of compassionate love: therapists and other species.

Compassionate Love from Healers

Just because you pay someone to care about your well-being doesn't mean it's insincere. Therapists of any kind who care about healing and care about you—whether they are psychotherapists, massage therapists, or yoga therapists—receive far more than money in return. For most therapists, sincere and attentive caring is a calling and a mission. Therapists receive a deep sense of meaning, purpose, and fulfillment when they extend compassionate love to those they treat.

Above all, a healer dispenses kindness and compassion. Whether you call it *positive regard, responsive empathy,* or *unconditional therapeutic acceptance*, it may be the most important part of therapy and counseling.

Therapeutic compassionate love is different from other kinds of love. It's not like the love of a life partner, parent, friend, sibling, or child.* Healer love has clear and describable characteristics:

---

* If any of those types of love arise in the healer, it is called *countertransference*. It means that the therapist is distorting the relationship with his or her own unmet needs or with unresolved issues carried over from other relationships. For a therapist to be effective, he or she must examine and resolve those issues in personal therapy in order to be present in the therapeutic relationship with pure, undistorted caring.

- Listening attentively without negative judgment
- Being present with warmth and caring
- Encouraging clients to meet their needs in ways that are not harmful
- Gently but firmly pointing out self-destructive attitudes and behaviors
- Acknowledging the inner goodness and loving nature of the client
- Being tolerant and caring while maintaining an environment of safety and respect

The healing therapist provides this stance of compassionate love with nothing but payment expected in return. Such a position is not easy to learn and maintain, but it is immensely helpful to the client and fulfilling for the therapist.

Compassionate Love from Other Species

More than 62 percent of the households in the United States have pets. We have emotional support dogs (ESD), emotional support animals (ESA), mental health and psychiatric service dogs, and therapy dogs. Dogs show up in hospitals and sometimes in therapists' offices as healing assistants.[43]

Interacting with a pet raises oxytocin levels and lowers heart rate and blood pressure, and it lowers self-reported fear and anxiety.[44, 45] People who own pets were also found to have less isolating behavior (even if they didn't walk their pets). Spending time with pets leads to spending more time with humans, which increases the odds for finding compassionate love.

Compassionate love crosses all species: dogs, cats, horses, and birds. All are capable of receiving and giving love. For many humans, their significant other is a member of another species. Even in the wild, there have been reports of compassionate love extended to humans. Wild dolphins have rescued drowning people and saved them from sharks. Dogs and cats were wild before they became domesticated, and a lot of birds still are. The first scientific study of cross-species empathy showed that humans and domestic dogs responded with elevated cortisol (stress hormone) levels and similar behaviors (looking upset) when they heard crying human babies.[46] Clearly, other species are capable of delivering what we humans experience as compassionate love. Having a pet that you can love and that can love you can enhance your flow of healing.

Lisa's Compassionate Dog Love

Lisa was heartbroken. She had just learned on a social media site that Jake was going on a romantic cruise with a mutual friend from their high school days. For her it was the last straw.

"How could he?" Lisa wailed to no one in her empty apartment. "I thought we were closer than that. I thought he was committed to deepening our relationship!"

Jake's betrayal on top of Lisa's other stressors was too much for her to bear. Her father's death had been followed by her mother's, and then her brother had stopped communicating. Her business was having some difficulties, and she was afraid she couldn't pay the rent on the expensive and hard-to-get business lease she had just secured.

She was lost in a sea of hopeless misery as she held her knees and rocked against the wall of her living room. Her tears were endless, and her despair was bottomless. She was between life and death.

Her rhythmic rocking and wailing were interrupted by a wet sensation on her face.

What was happening? What could possibly be interrupting her descent into blackness?

She tried to see, but the world was a blur. She tried to hear, but she didn't really care.

As she returned to her darkness, the sensation on her face became more insistent.

It was Ginger licking her tears away.

Lisa tried to shake her off.

Ginger's licking became more insistent.

Lisa relented and grabbed onto Ginger's neck. Ginger sat down, and her wagging tail brushed dust bunnies across the floor.

"Thank you, Ginger," Lisa cried. "Thank you, God, for bringing me Ginger," Lisa wailed to her ceiling.

Her sobs began to quiet as Lisa held Ginger and rocked with her.

Ginger was all she needed in that moment. It has been said that a dog's saliva has antibiotic properties that have saved the lives of their injured owners. In this case Ginger's compassionate love was saving the soul of her beloved owner, Lisa.

Ginger's compassionate love awakened Lisa's own. As she petted Ginger, Lisa told her she loved her.

"Thank you, sweet angel," she said. "How lucky I am to have you in my life!"

Ginger looked at Lisa with her woeful eyes and licked her face again.

Lisa laughed and cried at the same time.

"Look at us, Ginger. Aren't we a sorry sight? And what kind of owner am I? I've neglected you all day, and still you come and comfort me. You are a dream come true!"

Ginger wagged her tail, sat up straight, and woofed at Lisa.

"Okay, Ginger, let's go for a walk and get you your favorite treat at the corner market."

On special occasions Lisa would stop at the butcher shop for a meaty bone full of luscious marrow for Ginger. Lisa decided that tonight would be just the night for such a treat.

Layer Two

Guidance

If enhancing your healing with Layer One's wellness approaches is not enough to resolve your anxiety or depression, you may need a therapist's healing guidance. Many caring and skillful people have devoted their careers to helping people resolve their emotional distress, and it's likely one of them can help you.

There are more types of therapeutic guidance than you may realize. I've divided them into three main categories: conscious guidance, body and energy work, and spiritual guidance. Some people engage in one type of therapeutic guidance, while others find that combining approaches accelerates their healing process. I recommend that you keep an open mind about what might help you. If one approach does not suit you, try another.

CHAPTER 7

Conscious Guidance
Psychotherapy and Counseling

Keep searching for yourself.
You'll find a wonderful person.

*I*f you're still feeling anxious or depressed despite following the suggestions I've made in Layer One: Enhancement, then you may need to reach out to a therapist for help. Working with an attentive, caring person who is equipped with skills to help you find your way can be a tremendous relief. A knowledgeable therapist can guide you and your flow of healing for short-term relief as well as long-term resolution of your distress.

Here are some reasons you might have for seeking therapeutic guidance:

- You need to find a way to lower your anxiety and you don't know how.

- You feel overwhelmed by emptiness.
- You don't want to take the antidepressant that your primary care prescriber gave you.
- You have a self-sacrifice/resentment cycle you'd like to break.
- You're constructing a wall of hatred with someone, and you'd like it to stop.
- You're having trouble managing food, sex, money, alcohol, or drugs.
- You're so worried about your troubled sibling, parent, or child that you're not taking care of your own needs.
- You're afraid that your level of sadness or worry is getting out of hand.

Any of the types of guidance I describe in this and the next two chapters can help with these and other issues.

How Psychotherapy Can Help You Heal

Psychotherapy is a direct and intentional method of resolving anxiety and depression. Psychotherapy enhances awareness and resolves pain and conflict through direct discussion and reflection.

Some people think psychotherapy is a friendly conversation. That's true, but it involves more than amicable banter. Psychotherapy, when done well, can result in psychological and emotional improvements that last long after the therapy has ended. In some cases, psychotherapy can permanently cure cases of anxiety or depression.

Whereas most pharmacological treatments for anxiety and depression may give temporary relief, the benefits of psychotherapy can last a lifetime. In addition, psychotherapy can produce the heightened wisdom and awareness that come with an examined life.

Just as a skillful parent guides the development of a growing child, so does a skillful therapist guide the flow of healing for a troubled client. Although your flow of healing is continuous and relentless, it sometimes hits an impediment or becomes derailed by misperceptions and unskillful responses in important relationships. A skillful therapist will help you see yourself and others as you and they truly are in order to help you resolve your emotional obstacles.

Psychotherapy Is a Brain-Altering Experience

Just as you can change your mind, so can you change your brain. The concept that the adult brain is fully formed and unchangeable is wrong. Psychotherapy can change how your brain works and even how it looks.

Centuries of neuroscience research support the capacity of your brain's ability to change. In 1793, Michele Vicenzo Malacarne, an Italian anatomist, described changes he induced in the brains of animals he studied.[47] After training one of a pair of animals, he dissected their brains. He found that the cerebellum of the animal that had been trained to perform complex behaviors was larger than that of the same type and age of animal that had not been trained. The significance of this finding was not appreciated for a long time.

Years later, the term *neuroplasticity* was coined by Jerzy Konorski, a Polish neurophysiologist, who furthered the work of Ivan Pavlov (of Pavlov's dog fame). Konorski described "plastic changes" in the formation of new synaptic junctions between nerve cells in his 1948 book *Conditioned Reflexes and Neuron Organization.*[48] The plastic changes Dr. Konorski discovered resulted from training he gave his subject animals.

The concept of neuroplasticity provides a way to understand how your brain can heal on a cellular level. Neuroplasticity also provides a model for understanding how your brain can be guided on its path of healing.

> Some people say they can feel their brain changing. With the effort of concentration, healthy repetition, or emotional release, the patterns and pathways in your brain become remodeled. You can even add brain cells in important locations.
>
> I knew my brain was changing in medical school. I just didn't know how. Finally I discovered that someone was able to study the brains of medical students (without having to dissect them!). Draganski and associates used MRI imaging before, during, and after medical students studied for a batch of especially difficult exams. Within months, the gray matter of the posterior and lateral parietal cortexes had increased significantly.[49]

Many studies have shown how psychotherapy changes the brain. With brain scans taken before and after psychotherapy, researchers have demonstrated which kinds of therapy affect different brain structures.[50] Psychotherapy can actually increase the size of your amygdala and hippocampus, areas of the brain involved in memory and emotional processing.[51]

Is Psychotherapy as Good as Medicine?

Psychotherapy is considered an effective form of medical treatment by many influential people in medicine, mental health, insurance, and policymaking. The studies that show psychotherapy's effectiveness and its effects on the brain have given psychotherapy credibility in the eyes of scientists and health insurance providers.

In a sixteen-week study of treatment of moderate to severe depression, antidepressants were compared to cognitive behavioral therapy (CBT). After sixteen weeks, 57.5 percent of the people treated with medicine had a good effect compared to 58.3 percent of those treated with therapy.[52] In this study, therapy was just as good as medicine after four months.

The researchers went a step further. After the four months of treatment, they stopped treatment with both medicine and therapy. Then they went back a year later to see how the subjects were doing. Of those who had taken medicine, 76 percent had relapsed into clinical depression at the one-year mark. Of those who had received psychotherapy, only 31 percent relapsed. The psychotherapy group did more than twice as well as the medicine group, showing that therapy had a lasting effect while medicine did not.[53]

A huge study from a British journal compared various medicines to psychotherapy for social anxiety. They studied 13,000 patients from 101 studies. They found that psychotherapy was just as good as medicine but without the side effects and relapse problems encountered with medicine.[54]

People who suffer with posttraumatic stress disorder (PTSD) may also achieve long-lasting results with psychotherapy without

the side effects of medicine. In an Israeli study, subjects who suffered trauma-related symptoms (flashbacks, nightmares, and
exaggerated startle) did much better with CBT than with escitalo-
pram (brand name Lexapro).[55] The people in the two groups were
treated for twelve weeks and tested for results at the five-month
mark. Two months after the treatments had ended, the researchers found that 62 percent of the people treated with medicine still
had symptoms of PTSD, but only 18 percent of those treated with
therapy alone still did. Another study compared medicine to CBT
for obsessive-compulsive disorder (OCD). They found that eight
weeks of twice-weekly psychotherapy treatment with cognitive
behavioral therapy produced better results than eight weeks of
medication treatment with risperidone, an antipsychotic that in
low doses helps OCD. Cognitive behavioral therapy required more
time and effort than swallowing a pill but did not cause side effects,
and psychotherapy resulted in longer-lasting improvements than
medication.[56]

Studies have also shown that psychotherapy added to medicine works better than medicine alone. A study in the prestigious
New England Journal of Medicine reported that chronic depression
responded just the same to medicine and to psychotherapy (48 percent for each). When combined, however, a remarkable 73 percent of
people responded well.[57] As a result of this and other studies, many
prescribers insist that their patients engage in psychotherapy along
with taking medicine.

Although research studies have shown that psychotherapy often works better than medicine, sometimes the symptoms of anxiety or depression are so severe that psychotherapy alone is not enough. If you find yourself in so much distress that you cannot make effective use of therapy or seem to derive no relief from it, medication may help. Be aware, however, that too much or the wrong kind of medication can interfere with psychotherapy by suppressing your feelings. Brain blunting by medicine can delay mind healing with psychotherapy. You'll learn more about when medicine might help and how to safely add medicine to your healing plan in Layer Three: Restoration.

What Kind of
Therapy Should You Have?

Just as there are many types of diet, exercise, and meditation, there are many types of therapy. As you read my descriptions of the different types, take time to check how you feel about them. If a particular type of therapy seems right for you, it may make sense to try it.

An experienced therapist will usually know whether his or her approach will help you. No matter what type of therapy you choose, working with someone who is well trained and well experienced is at least as important as the type of therapy offered.

Just as important is how you feel about the therapist. Does this person feel like the right match? Does he or she seem kind, knowledgeable, and respectful? Do you feel you can share embarrassing information without being judged? If you don't feel this way, discuss it with your therapist or try someone else.

Although many types of psychotherapy are available, here are six of the most popular:

- Psychodynamic psychotherapy
- Cognitive behavioral therapy (CBT)
- Group therapy
- EMDR (eye movement desensitization and reprocessing)
- Addiction counseling
- Codependency counseling

Psychodynamic Psychotherapy

Psychodynamic psychotherapy is sometimes called *insight-oriented therapy* or *supportive/expressive therapy*. It is the main focus of the work that most therapists do when they say they are "eclectic." *Eclectic* means they know how to do more than one type of therapy, and they will offer you whichever ones they think will be most helpful. An eclectic psychotherapist might offer cognitive behavioral techniques to help you extinguish a compulsive behavior or address an addiction problem with motivational techniques. If you suffer with codependency and fear other people's anger, an eclectic psychotherapist might suggest you role-play what you would say to someone during a confrontation. With traditional psychodynamic psychotherapy, a therapist would encourage you to see how experiences in your past can distort how you see and respond to situations in your life today. Seeing how you can misread someone's intentions can lead to healthier perceptions of and responses within your most important relationships.

For example, if you had a mean parent, you may be unnecessarily timid or overly reactive in your current relationships. If you felt abandoned when you were a child, you may find yourself in a series of relationships with people who seem to be cold and distant or inconsiderate of your needs.

As you develop awareness and insight about your earlier patterns, you may see how you repeat them in your current relationships. You may be repeating unhealthy relationship patterns because you subconsciously choose mean, distant, or smothering people, or relationship problems may arise because you unwittingly and subtly encourage unkind behaviors in others.

A talented psychodynamic psychotherapist can help you connect the dots between what happened in your childhood and how things might be going poorly for you now. Your therapist helps you see how you may be superimposing your childhood experiences on your present-day relationships. With greater awareness of the nature of your childhood relationships, you'll be less likely to misread what is happening to you as an adult. Your responses in relationships will be based on what is actually happening rather than on how you expect things to be.

Psychodynamic psychotherapy is like orthodontia. It gradually aligns your perceptions with reality and leads you to respond differently and more skillfully. Just as an orthodontist gradually coaxes teeth into more effective positions, so does a psychodynamic psychotherapist help you shift perceptions and responses. Like orthodontia, psychotherapy can be uncomfortable at times, but short-term discomfort is followed by long-term change and improvement. Both orthodontia and psychodynamic psychotherapy take about the same length of time to accomplish and have lasting results. Going back occasionally for psychotherapy visits (tune-ups) can work like an orthodontic retainer.

Cognitive Behavioral Therapy (CBT)

Cognitive behavioral therapy (CBT) is popular with some therapists and social scientists because it is fairly straightforward and has easily measurable results. CBT is based on the premise that how you *think* about yourself affects how you *feel* about yourself. This form of therapy was initially developed to treat depression. If you substitute negative thoughts about yourself with positive ones, you are likely to feel less depressed.

CBT has been found effective for more than improving your self-esteem. It can be remarkably effective for anxiety conditions, including panic, phobia, and obsessive-compulsive disorder. CBT sometimes begins with teaching you how to relax your muscles. Relaxation exercises often involve visualization of peaceful times or places while you progressively relax all your muscles from your toes to your scalp (or vice versa). Your CBT practitioner then encourages you to visualize scary situations while relaxing in order to become less fearful of them. Then, progressively, the therapist may have you experience a situation you fear while you relax your muscles. This is called exposure/response prevention (EX/RP). Presume that air travel frightens you; a therapist would have you imagine getting on an airplane, then going to an airport, and finally taking a flight.

Some people favor the pragmatic approach of using CBT to target symptoms and work toward symptom eradication. They find that the relaxation exercises provide quick relief and that CBT provides long-term effectiveness.

Many studies have compared the effectiveness of psychodynamic psychotherapy to that of cognitive behavioral therapy. Following an extensive review of twenty-three studies involving nearly 3,000 patients, the authors concluded that psychodynamic psychotherapy and cognitive behavioral therapy are equally effective.[58] Patients suffering with anxiety or depression and treated with psychodynamic psychotherapy did just as well as those with anxiety or depression who were treated with cognitive behavioral therapy. Based on these and similar findings, researchers suggest that if you do not experience relief with one type of psychotherapy, you may have a better outcome with another.[59]

Psychodynamic Psychotherapy	Cognitive Behavioral Therapy (CBT)
Seeks historic causes of misperceptions and repetitive unsuccessful behaviors	Focuses on how negative distorted thoughts and behaviors cause distress
Incorporates elements of support and expression of feelings	Replaces negative self-perceptions with positive ones
May include suggestions for assertiveness and other self-caring behaviors	Instruction often given for relaxation exercises and calming visual imagery
Increases awareness of how past experiences influence present perceptions and responses	Focuses on present problems more than past
Encourages realistic perceptions and responses	May include gradual exposure to feared situations while desensitizing anxiety
Usually long term	Usually short term

Lisa's Love Dysfunction

Lisa came into her session looking down and sad. I asked her what was wrong.

"I feel so alone. Like there is no one who cares."

I said, "So who in your life has there been, and who is there now?"

Lisa starting weeping.

"I miss my mother. I miss her so much. She was always there for me."

"Anyone else?" I asked.

"Yes. Uncle Kevin, my mother's brother. He calls me at least once a week to check on me. All my life, he's been there for me. He was nicer to me than my own father. I think he cared more, too."

"Anyone else?"

"Yes. Ginger. She came into my life when my father was dying. I know she's just a dog, but the way she looks at me, I think she understands. She comforts me when I'm sad, and she's playful just when I need it. She doesn't mind if I wake her up, and she likes to cuddle."

"She's more than a dog," I said. "She's been the one constant in your home life through the death of your father, the death of your mother, and the other losses and stressors you've suffered. You saved her from the pound, and she saved you from despair."

"I thank God for Ginger every day," Lisa sobbed.

"How about your friend Rachel?"

"She's okay. She may be my best friend, but I just have to be careful about how much I can expect from her. She can be a little competitive with fashion and with men."

"What about men?" I asked.

"That hasn't been easy. Every time I get to know someone, they turn out to be mean or deceptive. I'm tired of men being apathetic, and I'm tired of them cheating on me."

"Like your father?"

"Yes, Dr. Freud. Like my father. Will I ever get over it and find someone who's nice to me?"

"What about Jake?" I asked.

"Jake is awesome. He's been a good friend since high school. Even though our relationship with each other has been on and off, we recently reconnected."

"Do you think anything will come of it?" I asked.

"What do you mean? Like sex? He's a friend with benefits, if that's what you mean."

"Do you think it's serious?" I asked.

"It's seriously good sex, and he's nice to me," she said.

"So, he's kind?"

"Very! And respectful! Sometimes I just want to snuggle and don't want to have sex. Even if he's hard, he's never pushy. He's able to hold me and fall asleep with me. That's a turn-on for my heart; I've always felt loved and accepted by Jake."

"Do you spend much time together?"

"Not as much as he wants to. I don't want to get too close because I'm afraid he'll change or leave. It always seems to go that way for me. Besides, he has a girlfriend, and I'm seeing someone else."

"Do they know?"

Group Therapy

I feel passionate about group therapy because I've seen it accelerate the gains my patients make in individual therapy. It can be especially helpful for anyone who is emotionally repressed or afraid of speaking up for herself. After experiencing group therapy myself and after leading two experiential psychodrama groups for fifteen years, I can assure you it's invigorating, exhausting, and intensely meaningful to be a group therapy participant as well as a group therapy leader.

Two of the most valuable ingredients of group therapy are witnessing and compassion. When group members witness one another's fears and losses, they become real and valid. The person expressing the fears and losses feels accepted and worthy of respect and lovingkindness. This experience gives authenticity to the group member's emotional world, and the person feels relief and hope as a result. The compassion expressed to a fellow group member fills both the sender and the receiver with love and self-respect.

As a group therapy leader, I was challenged, humbled, and inspired by the courage and determination of those who participated in the groups I led. Their willingness to dig the dirt out of their wounds and cleanse themselves of it inspired me. I was filled with respect, admiration, and love for those courageous souls who struggled their way to wellness.

Although acceptance and encouragement happen in individual psychotherapy, the support and fellowship of group represent the anesthesia that lessens the pain of self-exposure. Accessing, reexperiencing, and reframing the pains of your past in a group setting can accelerate your personal healing. Your fellow travelers in a therapy group can help you see the cause of your pain and how you can work your way out of it. Seeing how you can misinterpret the feelings and intentions of others in real time in a group setting can help you improve your relationships outside group. You become less apt to respond to others based on beliefs and expectations constructed from your past, and you become more likely to respond to others based on what they actually mean.

I have a personal passion for group therapy because it worked well for me. Having grown up in a physically violent and emotionally traumatic environment, I needed to find a way to heal my wounds. I tried face-to-face psychotherapy. It was interesting and very helpful. Then I tried psychoanalysis (five days a week on the couch). It was tedious, cerebral, and somewhat helpful. Finally I tried group therapy, which was the type of conscious guidance that helped me the most. It took me out of my head and put me right into my gut. I went from thinking about my issues to feeling them.

Everyone has some type of therapy that helps the most. Group therapy was mine. The less cerebral and the more emotional I became in group, the more progress I made in healing. Although group therapy was conscious, directed work, the emotional releases and warm validations I experienced felt spiritually guided. Things began to make sense—not just in my head, but also in my heart. For me, it was more healing to feel in my heart and gut what was right and what was wrong than to understand it in my head.

EMDR

If you've experienced trauma in your life, eye movement desensitization and reprocessing (EMDR) might help you. EMDR is a clever and effective treatment for childhood as well as adulthood trauma. It's especially helpful when traumatic experiences were so terrible that it's hard to talk about them or even remember them. EMDR can help you retrieve repressed memories and work through them so that they'll stop hurting you.

A trauma memory can act like an abscess. If it's too much to handle, your mind might wall it off. Its toxic contents, like an infection, are separated and contained. Your mind protects you from feeling overwhelmed by making some of the trauma subconscious. That's how a repressed trauma is like an abscess: It's under the surface, and you're protected from having to deal with too much of it at once. The problem with both a walled-off infection and a sealed-away traumatic memory is that each can gradually leak out and cause you pain and debilitation.

There are three ways to deal with a physical abscess:

- Ignore it and hope it will go away.
- Gently use hot compresses to soften the area and coax it to drain.
- Apply a local anesthetic and then lance the abscess so it will drain immediately.

Where psychodynamic psychotherapy is like using hot compresses for an abscess, EMDR is more like using anesthesia and lancing it (without the scalpel). EMDR can be a relatively painless way to uncover, reprocess, and release emotions associated with memories of childhood or earlier adulthood trauma. Here's how it works:

You sit comfortably and look to the left and right while remembering an upsetting event. At the same time, you are encouraged to think about yourself in positive ways. Examples of positive self-talk include reflecting on how you are not to blame for having been abused or traumatized, how you mean well to others, that you are a good person, and that you are safe.

Thinking about a traumatic event and substituting positive thoughts about yourself is called *adaptive information processing*. It means you are integrating a lousy experience within the larger context of seeing yourself in a better way. When successful, adaptive information processing leads to lower anxiety and relief. The traumatic memory no longer holds destructive power over you. Quite often, additional memories of unresolved traumas surface and can be subsequently processed and laid to rest.

Bilateral stimulation is a technique that reduces anxiety and allows easier access of painful memories. You might be instructed to look back and forth at flashing lights. Sometimes headphones are used with sounds alternating from one side to the other, or a handheld device is used to alternately gently touch the backs of your hands with a vibrating or tapping sensation. Sometimes all three sources of bilateral stimulation are used simultaneously.

This technique was developed by Francine Shapiro, PhD, in the late 1980s. She noticed that her eyes moved rapidly without her intending it when she had upsetting thoughts. She then discovered that if she deliberately moved her eyes while thinking about something upsetting, she had less anxiety. She refined the eye movements and trauma reprocessing into the method we call EMDR.[60]

EMDR has been the subject of considerable scrutiny. Some clinicians are thrilled with it, and others[61] think it's no better than the methods used in standard CBT—using relaxation techniques and positive thoughts about yourself—to work through past traumas.

Most studies have shown EMDR to be as effective or more effective for trauma resolution than general supportive therapy. Doing some EMDR work parallel to the work being done in psychodynamic psychotherapy can help dissolve a trauma while ongoing psychodynamic psychotherapy continues.[62]

Childhood trauma usually responds less effectively than adult trauma to any type of treatment, including EMDR.[63] Trauma that happened long ago, especially in childhood, tends to be more hardened than more recent trauma. For this reason, EMDR sometimes takes longer or has to be repeated more often for childhood trauma than for adulthood trauma.

Addiction Counseling

Addiction can block you from being able to heal your mind. It can also derail, shorten, or even suddenly end your life. Addiction shows up in 50 percent of everyone who struggles with mind suffering.[64] If you experience substantial anxiety, depression, mood fluctuations, or concentration difficulties, be careful not to let your sources of self-comfort get out of hand.

If addiction is part of your struggle, you must manage it before addressing any other causes of your distress. Dealing directly with an addiction is more important than knowing what caused it. If you don't directly manage an addiction, it will take you over and cause its own problems. Because addiction assumes a life of its own, it must be taken seriously and addressed as a separate problem.

Addiction is the use of a substance or a behavior despite negative consequences arising from its use. If you have alcoholism, you'll still feel compelled to drink even if you've lost your license, your job, or your home. If you're a sex addict, you'll still feel compelled to look for novelty sex even if it's caused the loss of an important relationship or a job or if it's given you an infection or resulted in legal difficulties.

Active addiction is a juggernaut. It stops for nothing. The more momentum it gains, the stronger it becomes. It's like a parasite, taking over your will, your values, and your future. It can become more important than your job, your family, and even your life.

Because urges can become so intense and denial can become so strong, addiction can hijack your mind and your life. You can find yourself trapped in an endless loop of compelling urges. As soon as they are satisfied, addictive urges scream for more. The need to satisfy urges leads to lying, deception, rationalization, and minimization—all of which spin a web to entrap you. Because of denial, you try to ignore the seriousness of your addiction. Because of shame, your self-esteem is crushed and your wish for help can become a desperate whisper.

Many people don't turn for help with addiction until a shocking event happens. This is called *hitting bottom*. Hitting bottom is often the only way to eliminate denial and motivate action to get help. It is often said that an addict is not ready for help until hitting bottom. A bottom could be as simple as people saying they are concerned about you. It could also be a serious loss of job relationships or health, or a shocking legal consequence.

If you think you are developing a problem with a substance or a behavior, there's a good chance that you have or you will. Now is the time to address it. If you can't stop it on your own, get some help.

Addiction counseling tends to be practical and directive. Although it's helpful to know about your past, addiction counselors are more concerned with your present. They will want to know your pattern of use of addictive substances and behaviors and the problems they have created. Counselors will provide suggestions for establishing and maintaining abstinence. After that, they will want to talk about relapse prevention and sustaining sobriety.

A lifetime of recovery is necessary for those who live with addiction. Relapse befalls the unwary and nondiligent. A commitment to recovery is necessary to sustain abstinence. Stopping and staying stopped are vastly different. Addiction counseling's goal is to help you establish and sustain a sober lifestyle.

Twelve-Step Programs and Sponsors

A fundamental feature of recovery for many if not most addicts is fellowship in a twelve-step program. Most twelve-step recovery programs are largely spiritually based with reference to a "higher power." (More about this in chapter 9.) Although God is often mentioned, some people prefer to think of the recovery program itself, or nature, or healing as their higher power. Once a commitment is made to engage in recovery, it's advisable to find a sponsor—a member of the recovery program who guides you in your process of recovery. Sponsors are not paid—they volunteer their time and energy. Their reward is feeling good about helping while simultaneously strengthening their own recovery program.

A person who agrees to be your sponsor will expect you to abstain from active addiction, attend and participate in recovery meetings, and be honest about the status of your recovery, especially if you are at risk of having or if you have had a relapse into active addiction. It's perfectly fine to work with a counselor as well as a sponsor. In fact, most addiction counselors urge or even require their addict clients to find sponsors.

Codependency Counseling

I was raised in a family with secret addictions, so I am painfully aware of the toll that addiction can take on lives, lifestyles, and relationships. Just as an active addiction can wreak havoc on the addict, so can an active addiction wreak havoc on a family.

When you love someone who has an addiction, many questions arise: "Should I do something? Am I doing too much? Is it my fault? How can I keep my loved one alive or at work? Why can't I get them to stop drinking or drugging or shopping or sexing?"

Those who live with an active addict suffer considerably. Spouses, children, parents, lovers, and friends struggle with insecurity, self-recrimination, and sadness. Being emotionally close to an addict can lead to more worry about the addict than about yourself. It can cause you to put your own needs aside while you try to meet the needs of a person who might not care. This pattern is called *codependency*. The struggle to worry about and try to help someone who resents your intrusion can lead to panic, despair, and lack of self-care.

When someone is emotionally close to an active addict, life is not predictable. From one day or even one moment to the next, the attitudes and behaviors of the addict can swing from one extreme to the other. Unpredictable episodes of violence, abandonment, or smothering can be frustrating and terrifying. Like the addict, codependent people experience swings of emotions. No one can tell which end is up. For the addict, it often doesn't matter; for the codependent, it can be agonizing.

Unlike addiction counseling, codependency counseling takes the past strongly into consideration. In this way, it shares characteristics with psychodynamic psychotherapy. Codependency counseling differs in that the counselor often recommends readings and participation in codependency recovery meetings. Codependency counselors often incorporate role-play and assertiveness training in individual work, and they often recommend group codependency counseling.

Following the formation of Alcoholics Anonymous (AA) in 1935, a companion twelve-step recovery program called Al-Anon was created in 1951. Initially designed to meet the needs of suffering spouses of addicts, it has expanded to include children, adult children of addicts, and others. Like AA and other addiction recovery programs, Al-Anon and other codependency recovery programs (e.g., Adult Children of Alcoholics [ACOA], Co-Dependents Anonymous [CoDA], and Families Anonymous) can be found in most nations around the world. If you are involved in a recovery program, one of the delights of travel can be attending recovery meetings in different cities and even different countries. People in recovery are generally welcoming to anyone who wants to attend a meeting, no matter their language or background.

Codependency recovery usually combines a spiritually oriented program with codependency counseling. Letting go and trusting in a higher power to assist your natural healing process is part of spiritual codependency recovery. Learning how to abstain from self-sacrificial patterns of behavior and speak up for yourself is also part of codependency counseling.

Combining codependency counseling with a spiritually oriented recovery program gives codependents hope and a sense of direction. Painful effort is required for the codependent to identify her emotional state and make sense of it. "Who am I? What should I do?"

These questions gradually make sense as the codependent person struggles to identify needs in a forest of worry. If you are a recovering codependent, as you begin to discover who you are and what you need, your anxiety will lower, your depression will lift, and your wisdom will deepen.

Lisa's Next Step

"Does the person you're going out with know about Jake?" I asked.

"Yes and no. He knew I was seeing other people, but he didn't want any details."

"Knew?"

"Yes, we broke up. His name is Ted. He yelled at me too many times."

"Are you okay?"

"I guess so. He never hit me, but he was mean. He was fun in bed, but otherwise he was a lousy boyfriend."

"Not like Jake?"

"Right. Not like Jake. Ted was like most of the guys I've gone out with: self-absorbed, demanding, and emotionally unavailable."

"Do you think you'll see more of Jake?" I asked.

"I'm thinking about taking a break from Jake."

"Why?"

"I feel insecure around him."

"Why's that?"

"I'm afraid that if I get too close, he'll leave me. I feel needy when I'm with him."

"What will you do?"

"Rachel and I are planning a trip."

"Where will you go?"

"We're going to a health spa up north. There's lots of yoga, meditation, healthy food, Pilates, tai chi, and no alcohol and no men. Very different from our last trip."

"Sounds great! What was the last trip like?"

"It was a cruise for singles. We signed up at the last minute. There was lots of unhealthy food, lots of booze, and lots of men."

"You didn't enjoy it?"

"Things got a little out of hand. One night Rachel and I went dancing. We drank a lot—too much—and took two men back to our room. The guy I was with turned out to be married. Well, actually, Rachel and I made out with both of them, so I'm not sure which one admitted he was married. We decided not to have sex with them, and then they asked Rachel and me to fool around with each other. We kicked them out; then we giggled about it all night."

This was one of several episodes of heavy drinking Lisa reported. She'd managed to stop using cocaine, but alcohol was more difficult for her. Her drinking was the subject of several sessions. Lisa was aware of her risk for alcoholism, given her family history. I wondered if she was beginning to take her drinking more seriously.

"Why now the health spa and no alcohol? Are you considering AA?"

"No. I've been to some AA meetings, but I felt uncomfortable. They reminded me of my father and his drunken rages. The only meetings I go to are Adult Children of Alcoholics and Co-Dependents Anonymous meetings. Since many of the people in the meetings have

alcohol or drug problems, I hear a lot about sobriety."

"Has it changed your mind about drinking?"

"I don't know. Maybe. You talk about it a lot with me. Maybe that helps. I know drinking is risky for me, and I feel like I should watch it more closely. A week with no alcohol, no men, and some quality friend time sounds just right."

CHAPTER 8

Body and Energy Work

A tale of two anatomies

*U*nlike psychotherapy and counseling, body and energy work can have a big effect on your anxiety or depression with little need for you to talk. In fact, massage therapy, acupuncture, or yoga therapy are sometimes all that's needed to heal anxiety and depression. Unblocking and realigning your flow of energy and properly positioning your body parts might be enough to lift your spirit and quiet your fears.

If you find that properly aligning your body or energy systems (or both) results in relief, you may have saved yourself some time and struggle. Most people, however, find that they must put in the time and effort that psychotherapy requires in order to effectively and sustainably heal their anxiety or depression. If that is the case for you, body and energy work might still be helpful. They can complement and even accelerate the work you do in psychotherapy. In fact, your mind healing may not be complete without attending to proper alignment of your body and energy systems.

Muscles and Bones, Meridians and Chakras

Body and energy work is a tale of two anatomies. Although there is considerable overlap, energy work primarily engages meridians and chakras, and bodywork primarily involves muscles and bones. Both sets of anatomies have a long history of study, with detailed descriptions dating back thousands of years.

Human anatomy has been the object of artistic renditions and scientific descriptions for as long as we know. The human body in its proper proportions and alignments has been revered in the Sistine Chapel and in cave drawings. Students of human anatomy from medical schools to art institutes use detailed drawings to learn the muscles and bones and their proper positions. Practitioners of bodywork must know how the body is constructed in order to properly help heal your body and your mind.

Bodywork in the form of massage therapy dates back thousands of years. In Egypt, the tomb of Akmanthor—also known as the Tomb of the Physician—has paintings from 2330 BC showing two men receiving foot massages (now called reflexology). In India, textbooks of Ayurvedic healing practices, written between 1500 and 500 BC, describe touch therapy. And in China, *The Yellow Emperor's Inner Canon,* written sometime in the period from 475 BC to AD 220, describes massage techniques for specific ailments. Caring people have been rubbing away one another's hurts for a very long time.

Energy work uses the anatomy of meridians and chakras, streams and collections of energy called *qi* (also spelled *chi* and pronounced "chee") that flow in and around your physical body. *Qi* is also known as the *vital force, life force,* or *life energy.* It is the precious energy of life that keeps you going. Long ago in the East, many practitioners thought it more important to work directly with vital energy rather than tinker with the body. They created detailed drawings and descriptions of energy anatomy and described how it must remain open and flowing in order to maintain good health.

Healing practitioners who work with meridians and chakras refer to drawings of energy anatomy, which is often shown overlapping with physical anatomy, so that the energy can be easily located. Most energy anatomy exists within the space occupied by the physical body, but some extends beyond it.

Beautiful drawings of meridians and acupuncture points are found in the literature of the Ming dynasty (1368–1644). Detailed drawings of meridians have been found as far back as the *Yellow Emperor's Inner Canon.* There are even primitive drawings of acupuncture points from the Neolithic (stone) Age of prehistoric China.[65]

The chakra energy system was first described in ancient India in the *Vedas* (Books of Knowledge) from 1700 to 1100 BC. Chakras are considered part of ancient Hindu and tantric yoga traditions. The energy anatomy of these traditions includes the chakras (energy centers) and nadiis, or channels, through which the life force (*prana*) flows.[66]

Although developed from different traditions, the healing practices of acupuncture and yoga share important characteristics. They involve a nonphysical body, called the *subtle body.* They also describe how the vital force flows and how it can be directed or guided for the sake of healing.

Energy work and bodywork may not directly engage your conscious mind, but they can positively affect your mood. When performed skillfully, energy and body alignments can also affect how you see your world and how you interact with it. If it appeals to you, body and energy work may be worth exploring.

Therapeutic Massage: The Body Remembers What the Mind Forgets

Therapeutic massage is used to treat many conditions, including anxiety and depression. Students of therapeutic massage become acquainted with physical and energy anatomy. Although most of their work is with muscles and bones, some of what they do involves acupressure (meridians) and positioning (chakras). Most massage therapists spend their time working to release tight muscles, but many are also capable and knowledgeable energy healers.

Muscle massage, even without deliberate acupressure, can produce surprising results for relief of anxiety and depression. Some massage therapists have witnessed the sudden release of emotion that comes with activation of a trauma memory. One of the most dramatic events in massage therapy, it can lead to dramatic gains in healing old wounds, reordering perceptions, and liberating pent-up energy. Muscle memory trauma release can happen unexpectedly in the course of massage therapy for depression, pain, or injury. At those times, although it may come as an unwelcome surprise, it is an unexpected bonus for healing the mind.

Muscle memory is something you count on when you walk, drive, ride a bicycle, or engage in other complex activities. It means you do not have to relearn these activities from scratch every time you do them. Since your muscles are connected to your brain, when you engage in activities with your muscles, memories can become activated. Along with memories, feelings can flood in.

Having the memory of a trauma released during massage can be tremendously healing. The mere outpouring of fear, anger, and sadness relieves a great burden. When combined with kindness and compassion, a corrective or reordering of perspective occurs. When a massage therapist uses kind touch along with compassion, greater self-acceptance and reduction of anxiety can result.

Lisa's Massage Meltdown

While she was away at a healing retreat, Lisa decided to have a massage.

Lisa's massage therapist was struck by the tightness in Lisa's shoulders.

"This will require some extra attention," she said.

As the massage therapist's knowledgeable hands began to relax Lisa's tight muscles, Lisa gave into the pleasant sensations and began to unwind.

This was a good idea, *she thought to herself.*

The massage therapist gently told Lisa that she would be moving up to Lisa's neck muscles. They were tight cords and needed some attention.

"Um huh," Lisa mumbled.

As her therapist began working with her neck muscles, Lisa stiffened and began to weep.

"Am I hurting you?" her therapist asked.

"No, it's okay," said Lisa. "I just feel sad."

As Lisa began to relax, however, a flood of painful memories overcame her. A flood of tears accompanied Lisa's outpouring of emotions. The message therapist stopped the massage and encouraged Lisa to talk about what she was feeling.

"I suddenly saw my father's angry face," she said. "He was drunk, and he was choking me! I only remembered him yelling at me when he was drunk, but now I realize he tried to choke me, and then he slapped me!"

Lisa began to sob.

Her massage therapist gave her tissues and talked to her about what she remembered. She told Lisa that she was safe and that no one could hurt her. Then she asked Lisa if she wanted to talk about it.

Lisa told her more about her father's abusiveness.

Her therapist told Lisa that what happened was not her fault and that she's a good person. Lisa cried tears of relief.

Lisa's trauma release and her massage therapist's response to it illustrate two of the principles of effective trauma work: releasing and reframing. Step one is to find and express the trauma memory. Step two is to reprocess it from a safe, realistic, and encouraging perspective. By telling Lisa it was not her fault and that she's a good person, the massage therapist helped Lisa to see herself and the traumatic incident in a healthier way.

It can be transformative to have this kind of shocking realization and to release the feelings around it. Lisa had the courage to accept this painful part of her past and let out her feelings in a safe and supportive context.

Although trauma releasing and reframing is not the intended goal of massage therapy, it occasionally happens. Massage therapy more typically results in mind healing in a subtler and less dramatic way.

Effectiveness of Routine Massage Therapy for Depression and Anxiety

Routine massage therapy can be just as effective as psychotherapy for depression and anxiety. In a 2004 meta-analysis, thirty-two studies were reviewed on the effectiveness of massage therapy for depression and anxiety. They found that even with a single dose (one massage session), 64 percent of the participants achieved a significant reduction of both anxiety and depression. When the subjects returned for multiple doses (massages), 77 percent of the participants had a substantial decrease in anxiety, and 73 percent had a substantial reduction of depression. The results were comparable to the benefits of psychotherapy.[67] Even in the absence of trauma release, routine massage therapy can play a powerful role in helping your mind to heal.

Acupuncture Helps You Connect the Dots

Several thousand years ago in ancient China, a very observant physician discovered that soldiers struck by arrows in specific locations sometimes enjoyed relief of other ailments. This led to using needles placed in the same locations to relieve the same ailments that the arrow strike cured. This is one of the ways acupuncture healing points were discovered.

It's difficult to argue against a system of treatment that has been in use for thousands of years. People have been using acupuncture that long because it works. Western medical schools and insurance companies have encouraged its use. Let's take a look at how it can help your mood.

More than 3,000 studies have been conducted on the effectiveness of acupuncture.[68] The studies that have focused on acupuncture for depression have been mixed but generally favorable. One large review[69] showed insufficient evidence that acupuncture helps depression, while another showed it to be helpful.[70] A review of eight well-constructed studies showed acupuncture to be an effective treatment for depression.[71] Another review of thirteen studies showed that acupuncture combined with antidepressants had a significantly better outcome than using antidepressants alone.[72]

Numerous research studies have shown that acupuncture can help reduce anxiety. In a very large review of many studies, researchers concluded that plenty of evidence supports the effectiveness of acupuncture for anxiety. Acupuncture was shown to be just as effective as cognitive behavioral therapy (CBT) in a comparison study.[73]

Acupuncture also did as well as CBT in a study comparing the two treatments for posttraumatic stress disorder (PTSD).[74] In the study, the people who received acupuncture did just as well as those who received CBT. The positive effect remained when people were checked again three months after their treatments. This suggests that acupuncture, like psychotherapy, may have lasting results. Acupuncture and psychotherapy both have this advantage over medication.

Acupuncture and Your Emotional System

Researchers have shown that parts of your brain are activated when acupuncture is used to help your mind to heal. One group found that the limbic system was strongly affected. Your limbic system, among its other functions, could be called your emotional system. It is the part of your brain that correlates most closely with your emotions, behaviors, and memories. Acupuncture needles, correctly placed, have been shown to affect this part of your brain in a way that helps your mind to heal.[75]

This finding was confirmed by another group of researchers, who found that the amygdala and hippocampus were strongly activated by correctly placed acupuncture needles.[76] The amygdala and hippocampus are the parts of your limbic system that have the strongest effect on your feelings. The researchers showed that acupuncture needles placed close to the correct acupuncture points had no effect. The hippocampus and amygdala portions of the limbic system were activated only when the needles were placed precisely where they needed to be.

A thorough knowledge of energy anatomy is essential for a well-trained doctor of acupuncture, and many acupuncture points assist in healing. You may ask if your acupuncturist is familiar with the points that help to reduce anxiety and depression.

Acupressure: Fingers Instead of Needles

Acupressure, like acupuncture, is an ancient Chinese healing practice that is studied and practiced worldwide. Acupressure addresses the same points on your body as acupuncture, but it uses finger pressure instead of needles. Acupressure has also been called *acupoint massage* and *Shiatsu*. Acupressure was also described in the *Yellow Emperor's Inner Canon*.

Acupressure may come naturally to you; you may even use acupressure on yourself without realizing it. When you feel stressed, you might unconsciously press your thumb and first finger on the bridge of your nose as if to squeeze the top of your nose. Or you might lean with your knuckle against the space between your eyebrows. Some people massage the muscle between their thumb and index finger.

These are acupressure points.[77] If you press them, you may feel some temporary relief of stress and anxiety. Acupressure, whether you administer it to yourself or it is part of a massage therapy session, can give quick relief.

Yoga Therapy

Aside from being a pleasant social activity and good for your body, yoga is good for your mind. Yoga is more than a good workout. It is increasingly recognized as a therapeutic technique. As a form of therapy, it has the capacity to guide your mind on its healing path in ways you may not have expected.

Using the positions (*asanas*) of yoga makes good common sense. Everyone knows it is a good idea to stretch and be flexible. You may be practicing your own form of yoga at times throughout the day just by stretching. Over the years, the positions of yoga have become more complex and refined. People discovered they felt better and healed faster if yoga was a part of their daily routine. When contemplative states of consciousness and intentional breathing patterns are incorporated with a series of bodily positions, yoga has even more power to heal.

Traditional yoga involves an energy system comprising seven primary chakras or energy centers. They are located roughly along your spine, in your forehead (the "third eye"), and on the crown of your head. When your chakras are aligned, opened, and flowing freely, your life energy is helping you to heal illness and stay healthy. Practitioners (yogis) describe great physical, emotional, and spiritual benefits in health and energy.

Most people think of yoga mats and difficult positions when

they think of yoga. Positions are an important part of yoga and yoga therapy. The positions move gradually from easy to more difficult. You should never push yourself too fast because this will cause pain and possibly injury. The goal with each *asana* is for you to come to peace with it. Although it may be difficult in the beginning, you will feel more balanced and comfortable with each position as you continue to practice it. Yoga is not a race, and there are no prizes but the reward of better health. Yoga also teaches a valuable lesson: taking on a challenging *asana* and coming to peace with it is like coming to peace with a challenging situation in your life.

Just as there are many types of psychotherapy, there are many schools of yoga. Most of them benefit your mind as well as your body. Three types of yoga have recently been shown to have therapeutic benefit for your mind beyond what you would expect from exercise and meditation.

Iyengar yoga, named after B. K. S. Iyengar, is a form of yoga that enhances strength, flexibility, and balance mainly with *asanas* and *pranayama* (breath control). It was studied as a therapeutic technique in a group of depressed people who had only a partial response to their antidepressant medication. Of the seventeen people who completed the classes, eleven had complete remission of their depression.[78] Yoga was thus demonstrated as an effective therapy for depression.

In another study, *shavasana* was used with depressed university students.[79] *Shavasana* is a position sometimes called the *corpse pose*. To perform *shavasana*, you lie on your back with your arms at a 45-degree angle. You close your eyes and breathe slowly and deeply. You scan your body for tense muscles and relax them. You then rid yourself of thought as you become aware of your breathing and enter a deeper state of mind.

The university students did well with it. Every one of them experienced reduction of depression compared to a group of control students who did not regularly perform *shavasana*.

In another remarkable study, Sudarshan Kirya yoga (SKY) was used alone in severely depressed people. SKY is a yogic breathing practice that uses various types of cyclical breathing patterns. SKY has been taught to more than 6 million people worldwide. In Western science terms, it appears to reduce depression by stimulating the vagus nerve. (In addition to reducing anxiety, direct vagus nerve electrical stimulation has been found to help treat depression.) It has also been suggested that SKY releases hormones like oxytocin that produce feelings of well-being. SKY has been shown to reduce cortisol (stress hormone) levels and raise serum brain-derived neurotrophic factor (BDNF) levels. Elevated BDNF levels correlate with relief of depression.

In the SKY study involving severely depressed people, yoga was compared to electroconvulsive therapy (ECT) and to imipramine, a powerful antidepressant. ECT did best with 93 percent of people achieving remission of depression—that is, becoming symptom free. The imipramine group came next at 73 percent. The big surprise was that the SKY group achieved 67 percent remission without any other treatment.[80]

I don't recommend that you count on SKY alone for a severe case of depression, but it might help boost the effectiveness of whatever else you are doing.

SKY has also been helpful for stress-related anxiety, depression, and insomnia following trauma. It has been used successfully for people experiencing these symptoms after wars, earthquakes, floods (the 2004 Southeast Asia tsunami), terrorism (the 9/11 attacks), and hurricanes (Katrina in New Orleans). It is said in SKY that rather than allowing emotions to alter your breath, use your breath to alter your emotions.

Whether you use a yoga practice that focuses on positions (*asanas*) or one that focuses on breathing (*pranayama*), you are likely to derive benefit from it. If you plan to use yoga to help your mind to heal, I recommend finding a yoga teacher with advanced training or a certified yoga therapist to help you.

Lisa's Yoga Healing

After her surprise revelation during massage therapy, Lisa decided that taking a yoga class might help to calm her. Discovering that her father had choked her during one of his drunken rages was a terrible shock. As compassionate and effective as the massage therapist had been, Lisa still felt stirred up and anxious. She was afraid she might have a panic attack. She asked Rachel to join her in a yoga session.

On their way to the session, Lisa thought about what she wanted to say to the teacher. It was a beautiful fall day. The leaves were just beginning to turn, and the view across the valley was magnificent. Lisa felt her shoulders loosen a little as she enjoyed watching a nuthatch hanging upside down by its feet on a birdfeeder. She still felt pressure from the unpleasant memory of abuse by her father, and she was glad Rachel was coming with her.

"He was worse than you thought, huh?" said Rachel softly.

"It was pretty bad," said Lisa. "I never knew what to expect. Would he be in a rage, sloppy drunk and affectionate, or sober and critical? Sometimes I think not knowing what to expect was the worst of it."

"*I remember a time when we were playing music in your base-ment,*" Rachel said. "*Your father came home from work in a foul mood. He started yelling at us to turn off the music and clean up the basement. You told me I should leave, but I didn't want you to be alone.*"

"*I could tell nothing worse would happen, and I didn't want you to get yelled at,*" said Lisa. "*You didn't do anything wrong, and you shouldn't have been yelled at.*"

"*Neither did you, Lisa. You were just being a happy teenager looking forward to your second date with Jake.*"

"*Thank God for you and for Jake,*" said Lisa. "*If I didn't have you in my life, I don't know what I would have done.*"

"*You know that I love you,*" said Rachel, "*and so does Jake. In fact, I think he loves you more than you realize.*"

"*Maybe I feel the same way about him,*" said Lisa. "*Since we have been seeing more of each other, it feels different . . . more serious somehow.*"

"*You've both had a lot to deal with and a lot to get over,*" said Rachel.

"*And obviously I still do,*" Lisa said as they walked up the steps to the cedar-sided yoga studio.

The teacher had gotten to know Lisa and Rachel during a couple of scheduled classes. She knew that they were well versed in the basics of hatha yoga and knowledgeable about chakras and their meaning.

When Lisa explained what had happened, the teacher agreed to do a private session for them. "*I think we should do a vinyasa—a combination of postures or asanas—that will open both your heart and throat chakras. Is that okay with you, Rachel?*"

"*Sure,*" Rachel said, "*if you think it will help Lisa.*"

After they completed a series of positions, including positions that focused on their throat chakras (energy centers), Lisa and Rachel made themselves comfortable, lying on the floor in shavasana position with their arms at 45-degree angles from their bodies. They took deep, slow breaths (deergha pranayama). They scanned their bodies for points of muscle tension and relaxed them. Lisa settled into a meditative state and directed energy to her throat chakra with her mind. When memories of her father choking her intruded, she shifted her attention to her breathing and went deeper with her meditation. After several cycles of this, she settled into a deeper state of near nonawareness. Spontaneously, her mind began to lift back toward consciousness. Eventually she began to flex her fingers and toes. Then she stretched her body and raised her knees to her chest. Then, in that same position, she gently rolled to her side. After a slow, deep breath, she sat up.

The light was different, and Rachel and the teacher were smiling at her with the sweetest looks of loving compassion.

"How long was I in shavasana?" Lisa asked, with tears forming in response to their loving-kindness.

"About an hour," the teacher said.

Rachel had finished her shavasana after about twenty minutes, and she and the teacher patiently and lovingly waited for Lisa, giving her the time she needed.

"How do you feel?" asked the teacher.

"Wow," said Lisa with misty eyes. "Open!"

Both Lisa and Rachel felt a tremendous lifting of tension and anxiety. Lisa felt like she could breathe more freely, and Rachel felt compelled to sing "Ain't No Mountain High Enough." As Rachel's beautiful voice rang clearly over the valley, Lisa cried tears of joy for all the love and beauty in her life.

CHAPTER 9

Spiritual Guidance

*Put yourself in a state of mind that
will invite a state of grace.*

*B*ecause you are a living being, you have already experienced the
power of healing. As you have grown and your cuts and scrapes
have healed, you have benefited from the natural process of healing
that directs your growth and makes you well. You did not create your
natural healing process. You benefit from it, but you are not its author.
All you can do is help it do its job.

You have already learned several ways to enhance and guide your
natural healing ability. Spiritual guidance is another way to help your
healing process stay on track. Spiritual guidance helps you synchro-
nize yourself with the powerful force that drives your growth and
healing.

There are many paths you can follow and many people are
available to help you deepen your spiritual life. Regardless of your

philosophical or political orientations, I hope you can find a way to deepen your spiritual experience.

Some choose to deepen their spiritual practice within the guiding structure of a religion. Others choose a twelve-step recovery program, nonreligious prayer sessions, or the help of a shaman. Plenty of evidence suggests that deepening your spiritual practice will help you on your path of healing. I've known people who declare themselves atheists who nonetheless have rich spiritual lives. Some of them commune with nature, and others find transcendence by meditating and being in the moment. Whatever your spiritual path may be, following it is likely to help you heal your anxiety or depression.

Spiritual Guidance with Religion

If you have a religion you feel good about, you may already be tapping into it to seek spiritual guidance. Using religion as a spiritual practice means more than going to church on Sunday or to temple on Saturday, or praying toward Mecca five times a day. Most religions have their own ideas about spiritual practice, and practice usually starts with prayer.

Embracing a spiritual practice within a religion can open doorways you may not have considered. Discussing it with your minister, priest, rabbi, or imam may be your next step. As you do, keep in mind the difference between religion and spirituality.

Most clergy people are deeply spiritual, and most can help you with your spiritual practice. Within clerical study is chaplaincy, the practice of helping people with their earthly lives as well as with their spiritual lives. Some clergy are so skillful that some of my patients and friends prefer to do conscious counseling with their pastor rather than with a psychotherapist. The combination of conscious guidance and spiritual guidance can be powerful and helpful.

Prayer Helps Healing

Plenty of evidence shows that prayer and participation in religious or other spiritual practices speed healing. Well over 1,000 scientific studies have shown a strong link between prayer and health.[81] Twenty-three studies on "distant healing" (prayer without touching the person) were reported in the *Annals of Internal Medicine*.[82] Thirteen of those studies (57 percent) showed "statistically significant treatment effects"—in other words, a positive effect from prayer. These results are superior to those in many studies of psychiatric medications.

Dawson Church, a psychologist and author of *The Genie in Your Genes*, summarized the results of many studies. He concluded, "In order for prayer and intentionality to be powerful, it must be deeply personal and sincerely engaged."[83] As you might expect, prayer works best when you really mean it.

A group of sociologists explored the idea that the power of prayer affects your degree of personal engagement.[84] They demonstrated that the nature of someone's relationship to one's idea of God has a strong bearing on the outcome, showing that praying to a kind, loving God results in greater relief of anxiety than praying to an angry, vengeful one.

Psychologist Lisa Miller and her colleagues reported in the *American Journal of Psychiatry* the results of a remarkable ten-year study of religion and depression.[85] Miller and her colleagues studied people who were at high risk of developing depression because of their strong family history. In the study they found a 90 percent reduction in risk if people reported that religion or spirituality was highly important to them. Having strong religious or spiritual feelings protected them from developing depression. Simply attending religious services was not enough, though. Those who attended religious activities but did not feel a strong spiritual connection did not derive the same benefit. A high personal importance placed on spirituality was needed for protection against a likely case of inherited depression.

The team went on to study the brains of their subjects with magnetic resonance imaging (MRI) after ten years of religious or spiritual affirmation. They discovered that people who placed a higher importance on religion or spirituality experienced greater cortical thickening, indicating improvement in brain structure, than did those for whom religion or spirituality was not important. The spiritual group had a thicker cortex in the medial (inner) wall of the left hemisphere of the brain, the same area where thinning was found in people who were at highest risk for developing genetic depression.[86] These remarkable researchers showed that religion and spirituality can protect against depression with measurable effects in the brain.

Twelve-Step Self-Help

The twelve-step self-help recovery program had its start with Alcoholics Anonymous (AA) in 1935. Like most organizations, AA had its progenitor. For AA, it was the Oxford Group. Doctor Bob, a recovering alcoholic, was involved in the Oxford Group in Ohio. Designed to address any type of emotional or mental suffering, it had a strong spiritual basis. The Oxford Group was not a clinical intervention but a social fellowship with an informal spiritual practice.

Dr. Bob introduced his friend and fellow alcoholic, Bill Wilson, to it. Together they modified and adapted it to the needs of the alcoholic. To call AA a modern-day miracle is not an exaggeration. Prior to AA, alcoholics were destined to be misdiagnosed, mistreated, misunderstood, and labeled as moral derelicts. The rates of recovery from alcoholism were abysmal. Becoming a "skid-row bum" was the frequent fate for many previously high-functioning alcoholics as the disease progressed. Alcoholics were often ostracized and abandoned by their families, and their lives often came to a painful and lonely end.

This situation began to change with AA. No longer did alcoholics have to rely on a system that mistreated them. There was finally an alternative to the naïve medical approach that misunderstood them. The fact that AA was a spiritually based program helped to ensure its separation from medicine.

Bill Wilson and Dr. Bob brilliantly fashioned the twelve steps and twelve traditions of AA. AA is so well designed, so long lasting, and so effective that its foundation seems to have been spiritually guided.

After AA was established, numerous other twelve-step programs followed. First came Al-Anon, the companion program for spouses and family members of alcoholics, which began formally in 1951. Both AA and Al-Anon have given rise to many more types of twelve-step programs. From AA came NA (Narcotics Anonymous), GA (Gamblers Anonymous), OA (Overeaters Anonymous or, more accurately, those for whom food is too important), SAA (Sex Addicts Anonymous), SLAA (Sex and/or Love Addicts Anonymous), and others. From Al-Anon came Alateen, ACoA (Adult Children of Alcoholics), CoDA (Co-Dependents Anonymous), and others.

There seems to be a twelve-step meeting for every form of overuse or overfunctioning—a welcome phenomenon. These nonreligious, spiritually based programs, which appeal to millions of people around the world, have been lifesavers.

Although God is referred to, participants are encouraged to use the term "higher power" if they are offended or uncomfortable with the term "God." For some, the higher power is the self-help program itself with its fellowship, philosophies, and helpful phrases. "One day at a time" and "Let go and let God" have become part of the language of our time. Millions have enjoyed the benefits of the phrases and the fellowship.

If you feel comfortable identifying yourself as an alcoholic or addict, you qualify for membership in a twelve-step program for addiction. If you're not comfortable with identifying yourself as an alcoholic or addict or if you're not sure you qualify, you can attend an open meeting, which welcomes addicts and nonaddicts. There are no dues for any twelve-step program, and you can find times and locations of meetings online.

For Al-Anon and other types of codependency recovery meetings, simply find one online and go there. I recommend trying more than one meeting as you may need to attend several before you begin to understand the message and until you find meetings that best meet your needs.

Shamanic Healing

After meeting a shaman in the Peruvian Amazon and watching him in action, I became intrigued. What was he doing during his ceremonies? Many of the people I saw while I was there complained of depression. He seemed to help them, and I became interested.

Shamanism is the oldest and the longest continuously practiced form of spiritually guided healing on our planet. Cave drawings greater than 30,000 years old depict shamanic healing ceremonies. One shows a figure who appears to shake an object while another figure is lying on the ground. It is likely to be a shaman treating an ailing tribe member. The rhythmic percussion of a rattle can help a shaman self-induce a trance state. The shaman then journeys in a nonordinary reality to find power animals and spirits to help heal a suffering client. Actions by a shaman that may seem purposeless actually engage a complex inner world. During a shamanic trance, the shaman is seeking and bringing healing energy to a stricken patient.[87]

To this day, shamanism is practiced worldwide. If you have ever been in a drumming or chanting circle, you may have experienced a degree of transport into a mildly or even deeply meditative or trancelike state. This is sometimes called *neo-shamanism*. Repetitive or monotonous percussion can facilitate, through a concept called *entrainment*, a nonordinary reality. Drummers, dancers, and singers have reported varying levels of meditative transport. When done deliberately and repetitively, drumming, chanting, and movement can lower anxiety and relieve depression. Some Western practices of music therapy and movement therapy are designed in this way to relieve anxiety and depression.

The ancient shamanic concept that all things are interconnected rings true to many people, no matter their religious background. Most spiritual traditions share a belief and faith in a divine interconnectedness. The concept of the interconnectedness of all beings and all things is at the core of shamanism. This has also been called *animism*: the belief that all things have a spiritual essence connecting them—including people, other creatures, plants, rocks, landforms, bodies of water, and spirit beings that we do not ordinarily see. Everything is part of the whole of natural substances, forces, and energies.

According to students of shamanism, this interconnectedness is what allows journeying to occur. A shamanic practitioner journeys by entering into a nonordinary reality and traveling to other realms. The three basic realms are the upper world, middle world, and lower world. In the lower world, a shaman requests the strength and wisdom of power animals. The middle world, a nonordinary version of our physical world, is where spirits reside. A shaman would go there to seek information and healing energy. The upper world is inhabited by teachers and helpers. A shaman would journey there for guidance.[88]

Although you may find some of those concepts unfamiliar or even far-fetched, many do not. The *Lancet Psychiatry*, a highly esteemed academic journal, took an interest in shamanic and other traditional healing activities, surveying thirty-two studies from twenty countries, many focused on shamanic healing. The authors concluded, "Traditional healers can provide an effective psychosocial intervention," pointing out that "traditional healers form a major part of the mental health workforce worldwide." The researchers concluded that traditional healers help common depression and anxiety but have less effectiveness with severe bipolar and psychotic disorders.[89]

Some people use shamanic practice for personal growth, self-development, or self-healing. Experienced shamans use their skills to heal someone else. Many years of study and practice are needed to be able to use shamanic journeying to help someone else safely and effectively. If you seek the help of a shaman, be sure that person is well trained and experienced.

During a shamanic healing journey, the shaman typically uses rhythmic percussion—music or dance—to enter a trance state.

Although some people use natural hallucinogens like ayahuasca or peyote to enter a nonordinary reality, many experienced shamanic healers advise against it. By using a psychedelic agent, you could lose perspective and make things worse. Most shamanic teachers advise their students to use monotonous percussion or other nonchemical forms of trance induction in order to remain in control during a journey and feel refreshed after it.[90] If you find the idea of working with a shaman appealing, I recommend that you work with someone who does not encourage you to use ayahuasca or other mind-altering drugs.

Everyday Shamanic Wellness

Shamanic healing doesn't have to be complicated. It can be as easy as a walk in the park.

You already know how good it can be for you to connect with nature. A walk in the woods, on the beach, or in a park can do wonders. Climbing out of your car, or getting away from your computer or your cubicle, and immersing yourself in nature is more than calming. It is healing. It refreshes your mind as well as your spirit as it aligns your inner nature with the nature around you.

This basic principle of shamanic healing through contact with nature can be enhanced by strong intention. In Japanese, it's called *shinrin-yoku*, roughly translated as the medicine of being in the forest. It has also been called *forest bathing*. Studies have shown it to have substantial health benefits.[91]

When you bathe in the forest or elsewhere in nature, take time to soak it in. Listen with your ears. See with your eyes. Feel with your skin and hair. Soak it into your pores. Breathe it into your spirit. Let your nature harmonize with the nature around it. Be still with nature and let yourself be healed by it.

Your Spiritual Path

When I suggest you develop your faith in healing, it is not because I want you to adopt an unproven delusion. The reason is that plenty of evidence shows that it works and that it helps you. Although belief in a higher power or a unifying force is not required for healing to work, plenty of evidence exists that such belief helps as well. Although there is merit in questioning why or how spiritual guidance works, there's a great deal of evidence that it has strong, positive effects.

Beyond the healing attitude of faith and the healing behavior of mindfulness, spiritual guidance helps you open yourself to the flow of healing that unites you with all other natural processes. The healing flow within you is connected to the great oneness. It is divine, and so are you.

Many people have a calling to help others study and practice spiritual healing. They become ministers, priests, shamans, and spiritually oriented counselors. You may seek a trained spiritual guide to help you develop your spiritual life, or you might prefer to deepen your spiritual connection on your own. You might deepen your spiritual connection in a church, a sweat lodge, a twelve-step meeting, or by walking in the woods. Developing yourself spiritually and engaging in a spiritual practice can help your healing flow to find its way. You don't need to believe in a deity to realize that, just as a flower miraculously blossoms, so can you.

Your Mind, Body, and Spirit Guidance Team

Having more than one type of therapy guide should not throw you off course as long as your therapy guides are on the same page and are willing to talk with each other if they need to. Just as it takes a village to raise a child, it can help to have a team of therapy guides to heal your mind. Whether your guides help your mind, body, or spirit does not matter as long as they are well trained and kind. Each type of healing guidance can complement the others.

Therapists, acupuncturists, and spiritual guides all have the same goal: to help you heal. Your minister, priest, or monk will complement your therapist as long as you let them know what is helping you and what is not. You are in charge of your healing plan and your healing team. Your healing guides need your feedback to know if what they are doing is helping.

When you choose a healing guide, the type of therapy or spiritual practice doesn't matter. Your choice should be based on what feels right and appears to be helpful. It should also be based on respect and genuine concern on the part of your healing guide. When these elements are in place, your guides are more likely to help your healing process find its way.

Jake and the Beanstalk

Growing up black in a wealthy white neighborhood was not easy for Jake. Too often people saw the color of his skin before they saw him. The exceptions were his childhood friends Lisa, Rachel, and Ray. Jake could feel their acceptance and love.

Jake's parents, who were professional athletes turned broadcasters, wanted Jake to have the advantages they missed growing up in a rough North Philadelphia neighborhood. They wanted their son to have a better start.

As an only child with ambitious parents, Jake struggled with loneliness, and he questioned his identity. While he was away at college, Jake enrolled in a course on West African drumming. There he felt accepted by the professor and by his fellow students. When he drummed in a group, Jake was transported to a state of bliss by the rhythmic energy of the drumming and by the camaraderie of his fellow drummers. He wondered if any of his ancestors might have been drummers.

Several years later while in medical school, Jake had a meltdown. He felt alone in the world and upset by the racist attitudes of the doctors at the teaching hospital. He questioned his choice of career.

Jake's friend Ray was living across town teaching anthropology at the main campus of the same university. The two friends met for lunch as they had been doing for several years.

"Why don't you try seeing a shaman?" asked Ray. "You love drumming and nature, and you said you may have had an ancestor in Africa who was a healer."

Jake surprised Ray by saying he had already met with a shaman and was finding it helpful. In fact, he had been dreaming more since meeting with the shaman. He shared this dream with Ray:

"I was floating in a forest of bean plants. Their stalks went on forever above me and below me. I couldn't see where they ended. They had no end. Then I realized I was a bud attached to one of the bean stalks. There were other buds on the stalk above and below me. Somehow I knew those buds were also me but at different times in the past and in the future. I knew I was just a small part of something much bigger. It was as if the stalk I was on went on forever, and each time I was a bud was just an instant. I felt myself become absorbed in the stalk, and then I would pop out as another bud as the bean stalk continued to grow.

"Then all the stalks were waving, flowing, and moving, mine along with them. It felt like they were communicating in some way I didn't understand. One of the stalks felt familiar. It felt as if it knew me. I felt content and happy in a way I never had."

Jake paused and asked, "So what do you make of it, Ray? Have you ever had a dream like that?"

"It sounds like shamanic journeying is paying off for you," Ray said. "That's a classic depiction of the soul. You came up with the beanstalk version. Now you know that you are part of your soul, which is limitless and connected to all other souls. I wonder what other soul felt familiar to you. How did you feel when you woke up?"

"Surprised," said Jake. "Surprised that the dream was so vivid. And I couldn't stop thinking about Lisa. Maybe it's time for me to get more serious about her."

"Maybe you should," said Ray. "You should follow your heart. What does your heart say?"

"I've always loved Lisa," said Jake, "but I've always been afraid to tell her. I've never thought I had a chance."

"Maybe your dream is telling you that you do. Maybe you should take a risk," said Ray.

On their way out of the restaurant, the two friends walked around an elderly Asian man sitting at a table. Next to him was a large burlap bag. He was pulling green beans from it, pinching off the ends, and throwing the beans on a pile on the table. The pile was so high that beans were spilling on the floor.

"How's that for validation?" said Ray. "Your beanstalk dream was just confirmed by a grandfather!"

Layer Three

Restoration

If your symptoms of anxiety or depression are so distracting that you cannot benefit from the wellness approaches of Layer One and the therapy approaches of Layer Two, you might need medicine to reduce your level of distress. I recommend you carefully consider whether medicine is a good idea before you start taking it. Aside from potentially dangerous side effects, medicine can blunt your emotions and slow your thinking, which can make it difficult for you to benefit from the possible long-term benefits of Layer Two. On the other hand, medicine can sometimes be lifesaving and life-style saving and should be considered when symptoms of severe depression or anxiety may be disabling or life threatening. To help you understand when medicine might be needed or helpful, I have created two categories: medicine for soft anxiety and depression, and medicine for hard anxiety and depression. Always be sure to consult with qualified professionals before you decide to start or to stop taking any medicine.

CHAPTER 10

Restoration with Medicine

Suffering accelerates healing.
Persistent misery can delay it.

Some types *of anxiety and depression* are genetic and hardwired and may not go away with enhancement and guidance alone. Other types, caused by trauma or persistent adversity, can also resist efforts to heal. Some conditions result in symptoms of anxiety and depression severe enough to immobilize the flow of healing. Panic or despair can be so bad that no amount of talk, exercise, or prayer will make it go away. When healing is blocked by symptoms too severe for enhancement and guidance to help, medicine can often restore the flow of healing.

Medicine for anxiety and depression should only be used when enhancement and guidance are not enough. Taking medicine when

191

it's not needed exposes you unnecessarily to side effects and can dampen feelings and thoughts, which makes talk therapy less effective. It could also delay your healing or pose a risk to your health.

Many people are reluctant to take medicine for anxiety or depression. Some fear its side effects. Others fear becoming overly reliant on the medicine or addicted to it. Some people fear being criticized or stigmatized for taking it. These reasons for caution or reluctance are understandable. Comparing the risk of taking a medicine to its potential benefit is very important. Comparing that risk to its potential benefit from the perspective of healing will help. Medicine is worth considering when it is likely to restore the flow of healing without causing serious side effects.

Should Medicine Be Part of Your Healing Plan?

Confusion about whether and when to use medicine is understandable. Many variables are involved in suffering, and many competing ideas are out there about how to help. What's needed is a rational perspective consistent with the goal of assisting the natural course of healing. When the question "Should I take medicine?" is approached from a healing model, your decision is more likely to be consistent with healing and growth—more likely to assist your healing than hinder it.

A gray zone exists between suffering that motivates healing and misery that blocks it. If you suffer too much, you might give up on yourself and your capacity to heal. If you medicate your distress away completely, you have no reason to seek guidance to resolve it. You could miss an opportunity for growth, wisdom, and contentment.

I'm not suggesting that you suffer unnecessarily. I'm suggesting that you tolerate a manageable degree of discomfort to identify problems and seek solutions. If you suffer too much, you may not be able to make good use of Layers One and Two. Medicine, when carefully chosen and used at the appropriate time, can restore your flow of healing by reducing severe distracting symptoms that block or derail it. Medicine can help when you are otherwise crippled by overwhelming and persistent suffering or distracting intrusive thoughts.

What Medicine Can and Cannot Do

Medicine won't eliminate trauma caused by childhood adversity, but medicine may reduce the symptoms enough for you to resolve the trauma with talk therapy and other types of guidance. If medicine reduces distracting symptoms enough for you to resolve your old wounds, you might then be able to continue your healing plan without it.

If your anxiety or depression is primarily genetic, medicine may reduce your symptoms enough for you to function and enjoy your life. It may also reduce your symptoms enough for you to more effectively address your current sources of distress and to resolve old wounds that may have previously felt insurmountable.

If you use medicine to reduce your symptoms of anxiety or depression, continuing to enhance and guide the flow of healing with Layers One and Two is still important. When medicine manages to reduce the intensity of distracting symptoms, enhancement and guidance of healing can more effectively empower and direct healing's flow. Studies have shown that medicine is more effective when combined with therapy.[92] Continuing to follow a proper diet, exercising, and managing stress can also improve your outlook and your outcome.

Medicine works only as long as you take it. If your symptoms remain resolved after you've stopped taking a medicine, enhancement and guidance may have helped you heal while you were taking it.

A Word of Caution

You or someone you know could be harmed by taking psychiatric medicine or by not taking it. Many variables affect the choice to take medicine and which one to take. So far, the science about those choices is limited. My hope is that by offering you a healing perspective about medication, it will help your choices to be safe and effective. Always discuss and consider your decisions carefully with the help of qualified professionals.

Overdoing Medicine

Too many prescribers and sufferers fall victim to the temptation of overdoing it with medicine, especially when the cause of anxiety or depression is too much stress or unresolved childhood adversity or trauma. These causes may be resolvable without medicine, and medicine could even hinder their resolution. Too much medicine or the wrong kind of medicine can cause *brain blunting*, which is when feelings are dampened and thoughts are slowed. Anesthetizing your feelings can reduce your suffering, but it can also prevent you from resolving its cause. Other unwanted effects—side effects— can include diminished sex drive or functioning, nausea, diarrhea, constipation, and other potentially troublesome or even dangerous reactions. When used incorrectly, medicine can cause serious problems in addition to blocking or derailing your flow of healing. These factors should be considered and discussed with a qualified professional before you decide whether to take medicine.

Consequences of Stopping a Medicine

The decision to start taking medicine for anxiety or depression isn't always an easy one, and stopping a medicine that has been helpful can be dangerous. If you have a genetic or other hardwired condition, you'll need to be extra careful. Some conditions have been present so long that they do not heal easily, and they can also fluctuate in intensity. If you have a hardwired condition, like genetically transmitted depression or bipolar disorder or if you have a history of severe or persistent adversity that does not respond easily to therapy, prematurely stopping medicine during a time of ease could lead to a relapse of symptoms, some of which could be sudden and severe. Stopping a medicine you need for severe depression could place you at risk for suicide. Before you make that decision, be sure to discuss with a professional the pros and cons of stopping a medicine.

When used effectively, medicine can save lives, jobs, and relationships. When the enhancement and guidance of healing are not enough to resolve suffering, the positive effects of medicine can keep your life and your healing on track. Keeping your healing process fully functional can help you discover and resolve your issues while you continue to engage effectively with your life. Medicine has limitations and drawbacks, but it can serve an important role in a comprehensive healing plan.

Medicine for Soft and
Hard Anxiety and Depression

Soft anxiety and depression are caused by adversity and trauma. They may also arise because of too much stress in your life. Soft does not mean easy; it means malleable—that is, the anxiety and depression can be changed like muscle size and tooth alignment. Soft anxiety and depression are problems caused mainly by situations outside your body. They affect how you see and respond to your world. Think of adversity and trauma as having caused software problems. Your brain and genes (your hardware) are functioning correctly, but your thoughts and emotions (your software) are not. Adversity and trauma can program your perceptions and responses by conditioning you to believe that troublesome circumstances in the past are being repeated in the present. Suffering caused by adversity or trauma is often resolvable with therapy or other types of guidance. Sometimes, however, adversity or trauma can cause so much pain that guidance alone can't help. That's when medicine might reduce your symptoms enough to get your healing back on track so that you can use therapy more effectively.

Unremitting adversity and trauma can sometimes cause changes in brain function and even brain structure that can be hard to alter with therapy alone. These hardened forms of anxiety and depression can even result in changes in genetic expression. These types of concerns do not respond easily to therapy alone, but they often respond well when medicine is added to therapy.

How to Determine When to Start or Stop Using Medicine for Anxiety or Depression

Deciding whether to start or stop taking a medicine is not easy. You should consider either decision carefully, discussing it with your therapist and prescriber.

Four Reasons to Start Taking a Medicine

If any of the following reasons describe your situation, medicine might restore your flow of healing so that you can make good use of Layer One: Enhancement and Layer Two: Guidance.

- You are so distracted by fear or despair that you can't have a meaningful conversation with a therapist about your problems.

- You are so burdened by distress that you can't start or sustain healing-enhancing behaviors such as exercise, a better diet, mindful reflection or meditation, and spending time with people who care about you.

- Your anxiety or depression is so severe that it jeopardizes your job or an important relationship, and therapy isn't helping fast enough.

- You have inherited or developed a type of anxiety or depression that is unlikely to get better without medicine. This can be difficult to determine because we don't yet have practical and reliable tests for genetic depression or anxiety. If, however, you have a strong family history of

depression or anxiety, genetics may play a role for you.
Aside from genetic inheritance, if you were subjected to
severe, persistent adversity or abuse earlier in your life,
you might have developed a hardened form of depression
or anxiety that might not respond to treatment without
medicine. (See more in chapter 12.)

Six Reasons to Stop Taking a Medicine

The following is a partial list of reasons to consider stopping
medicine for anxiety or depression. You may have other reasons of
your own. Any decision regarding medicine should be made after
consulting with qualified professionals.

- Medicine isn't helping because your level of distress is not
  severe enough for medicine to have a noticeable positive
  effect. If this seems to be the case, Layers One and Two
  may be all you'll need.
- A particular medicine isn't helping because it's the wrong
  one for your type of anxiety or depression. Although
  we have some genetic tests to help guide selection of a
  medication (see chapter 11), they are limited in scope.
  Prescribers currently rely mainly on symptoms, responses
  to medication taken in the past, and trial and error to
  determine what alternative medication to suggest.
- Though helpful, your medicine is causing gastrointestinal
  upset, impaired sexual functioning, or other unwanted
  effects that are worse than its benefits, and efforts to
  eliminate the medicine's unwanted side effects have failed.

If your medicine has been helping but also causing intolerable side effects, lowering the dosage or switching to a different medicine may be warranted.

- The medicine you take is blunting your emotions and slowing your thinking so much that you can't effectively use therapy or other types of guidance described in Layer Two. Be aware that if the medicine was helping, your symptoms could worsen or relapse. Lowering the dosage of the medicine rather than stopping it may be in order.

- Your medicine is causing addiction or placing you at risk of relapse of addiction. In particular, taking a high dose of a benzodiazepine—such as alprazolam (Xanax) or diazepam (Valium)—can result in addiction. It can also increase the risk of relapse to a previous addiction, like alcoholism or barbiturate or opiate addiction, by creating a sensation similar enough to the previous addiction to cause craving for the original addictive substance. If you are in recovery from a chemical addiction and medicine is absolutely needed for anxiety management, discuss safe choices with your counselor and prescriber.

- You are pregnant or trying to get pregnant. Although many medicines have been shown to be safe during pregnancy, as a general rule, I advise women not to take medicine during pregnancy unless their anxiety or depression is so severe that it interferes with their nutritional needs and those of their fetus. Medicine is often not needed during pregnancy because the hormones generated during pregnancy have antianxiety and antidepressant effects of their own. If, following delivery, a severe postpartum depression or a severe relapse of depression or anxiety occurs, medicine may be needed. If that is the case, then breastfeeding may not be advisable, depending on the type of medicine taken. Discuss these issues in detail with your obstetrician and with your prescriber if you're planning to get pregnant.

If you've been struggling with whether to take medicine, you're not alone. The use of medicine to help the mind heal is controversial and based on a blend of art and science. The suggestions in the following chapters are informed by scientific studies, which I apply to a healing model. My intent is to show you how medicine can be used to restore the natural flow of healing when suffering blocks it.

My fictional patient and your companion, Lisa, has struggled with whether to use medicine. Although initially opposed to the idea, Lisa learned how it could serve an important role in her healing plan. Along with discovering that she very likely has a case of hardwired genetic depression, Lisa struggled with painful emotions that blocked her capacity to exercise, eat well, and make good use of psychotherapy. Both factors—having hardwired depression and a blocked flow of healing—gave Lisa good reason to consider using medicine. Lisa has some good news about her decision and some surprising news that could change that decision.

Lisa's Big Surprise

Lisa's trip to a wellness spa with Rachel opened her heart in ways she couldn't imagine. Traumas she suffered in childhood had been nearly neutralized, and the insights she achieved at the spa helped to relieve her depression. Drinking alcohol was not allowed at the spa, and Lisa decided not to resume drinking upon her return home. This marked the end of Lisa's excessive use of alcohol.

Lisa has suffered with three types of depression at different times in her life: grief from the death of her parents, emptiness from childhood adversity, and possible genetic depression from her maternal grandfather (who killed himself when Lisa was five).

Of the three types of depression, grief was the easiest and most straightforward to resolve. Lisa needed to cry about it enough and talk about it enough to make her peace with it.

Lisa's second depression, emptiness caused by childhood adversity, was tougher to resolve. Fortunately, her newfound sobriety and unexpected trauma work laid more of it to rest than either she or I had expected. She still had residual hurts from her childhood wounds, but the worst of her traumas were resolved with the help of several types of guidance.

Lisa's third type of depression was likely genetic and still needed some work. Lisa had achieved a decent response to medication, but she and I were hoping for a full remission of symptoms, as sometimes can occur with medication given for hereditary depression. The last time we had met, she agreed to try a new antidepressant. I'd hoped it would deliver what she needed without the sexual side effects she had experienced from the last antidepressant she'd tried.

I could tell as soon as she walked into my office that something had changed. She was brighter and lighter than I had ever seen her.

"It looks like you're feeling better," I said.

"I am. I think the new antidepressant is working, along with some other changes in my life."

"Are you having any trouble with it?" I asked.

"Not so bad. Just a dry mouth and mild constipation. I've taken care of it with some dietary changes and over-the-counter remedies you suggested." She paused for a moment before continuing. "I'm pleased with the effect of the medicine . . . but what if I want to get pregnant?"

"Really?"

"Jake asked me to marry him, and we might want to start a family soon. After all, I'm not getting any younger."

"Wow! Congratulations! No problem! We will work out a safe solution for your future family."

"How?"

"The safest thing to do is to taper and stop all medication before you get pregnant," I explained. "Then we'll see how you do. If your genetic depression becomes unmanageable and threatens your safety or that of your fetus, you and I can work with your obstetrician or midwife to choose a medicine that will help relieve your symptoms so that you can maintain a healthy diet while posing minimal risk for your baby. Meanwhile, I suggest you continue to follow your healing plan with the enhancements and forms of guidance you've found most helpful."

"That sounds like a good plan," Lisa said. "I think Jake will be pleased. He's not keen on my taking medicine, even though he understands the medical necessity because of my genetic heritage."

"Don't worry," I said. "I think the nonmedicine part of your healing plan will be enough to keep you out of a severe relapse. Sometimes pregnancy itself confers some protection from depression. Are you using any birth control?"

"Yes, we are using barrier methods," Lisa said. "I don't want to confuse my head and body with extra hormones."

"It's going well?"

"Surprisingly well. I've always been in love with Jake, but I was afraid he didn't feel the same way. He told me he's always been in love with me but was afraid to get close."

"Why?" I asked.

"He was afraid of my father, and he was afraid of himself. He was afraid that he might hurt my father if he needed to protect me. He thought that could drive a wedge between us. Jake pulled away from me because it hurt him too much to see me suffering. He said he could be my friend, as we have been off and on, but he was afraid to open his heart to me."

"What changed?" I asked.

"My father died, and we both grew up," Lisa said. "I worked through a lot of my trauma, and Jake worked through a lot of his emptiness. He said the soul retrieval work he did with his shaman was helpful. I know the work I've done in group therapy and in other settings has made a difference for me."

"Have you set a wedding date?"

"Next summer. Jake will be finished with his fellowship and has already been asked to take a clinical research position with the medical school. He wants to treat patients and teach at the same time. He's really good at both. By then, I hope to have my yoga studio up and running. I'll be finished with my advanced teacher training and plan to teach classes and start doing yoga therapy. I'll keep the salon running, but my secret wish is to start a wellness center with a focus on healing. I want to help people be beautiful on the inside as well as on the outside."

"Great!" I said. "I look forward to referring people for both."

CHAPTER 11

Medicine for Soft Anxiety and Depression

A s mentioned in the previous chapter, soft does not mean easy; it means pliable. Soft anxiety and depression result from unreasonable stress or childhood adversity and trauma, two of the three causes of anxiety and depression discussed in chapter 2. For example, adverse childhood events can program you to expect the worst and to behave as if the worst is happening—even if it isn't. As a result, irrational fears combined with a low self-image give rise to symptoms of anxiety and depression. Most cases of soft anxiety and depression can be resolved by using Layer One: Enhancement and Layer Two: Guidance.

The goal in treating soft anxiety and depression is to use medicine only as long as it's absolutely necessary. Medicine's job is to reduce your symptoms long enough for Layers One and Two to work. Medicine may no longer be needed once enhancement and guidance have resolved enough of the issues that caused your suffering. Continuing to use medicine for a soft psychiatric condition when it is no longer needed can give you unnecessary side effects and delay your healing in a couple of ways:

- *Medicine can blunt your feelings and thoughts.* Taking medicine when you don't need it can delay or block the flow of healing. When your feelings are blunted, you have less motivation to resolve them with therapy. When your thinking is blunted, your mind has less capacity to make sense of the effects of childhood adversity or trauma on your current relationships and behaviors. Taking medicine when it's not needed for anxiety or depression can jeopardize the possibility of permanent resolution of your problems.
- *Medicine can cause physical side effects worse than its desired effects.* Gastrointestinal, sexual, cardiac, and other side effects can delay, derail, or block healing. Medicine can even endanger your health or your life. Learn about the possible side effects of medicine and discuss them with a knowledgeable professional.

Soft psychiatric conditions are caused by stress, adversity, and trauma. Exposure to considerable adversity can change your view of yourself and your world, leading you to see and expect the worst and making it hard for you to stay in the moment and enjoy your life. Resolving these issues with proper guidance is sometimes more efficiently accomplished with medicine. Let's explore whether using medicine may help you resolve old hurts or if it could actually impede your healing.

Should You Use Medicine?

Some people make the mistake of taking medicine too soon—before they give psychotherapy and other nonmedicinal approaches a chance to help. Mind healing takes time, maybe longer than you and those who care about you would like. It can also be more uncomfortable than anyone would like.

Psychotherapy is like orthodontia. Just as teeth move slowly with gentle but firm coaxing, minds do the same. The time frame for resolving adverse or traumatic childhood experiences, for example, is measured in months and years rather than days and weeks. Adding a medicine too soon risks blunting the feelings and thoughts needed to resolve issues that may linger from a difficult childhood. Permanent resolution of suffering is possible with time and diligence.

If, however, during the course of enhanced and guided healing for your mind, you become mired in *extreme* pain and suffering, you may need medicine to restore the flow of healing-promoting thoughts and feelings. Although knowing the right time to take medicine can be hard, if you are struggling without making headway, medicine could prove to be helpful.

How well you are functioning at work and at love is one way to gauge if it's time to consider medicine. If your job seems reasonably paced but you are not able to do it, you may be too distracted by distress. If you are not able to be present and engage in meaningful dialogue with your loved ones and friends, your distress may be interfering with your capacity to love. If these problems persist for several weeks or months, you may wish to consider taking medication to get your healing back on track.

First, though, be sure to discuss your concerns with the person providing guidance for your healing. She may first suggest adding a second type of psychotherapy or a different form of guidance (such as spiritual practice). It may help to review the steps you are taking to enhance your healing process. You might need to revise your meditation schedule or dial up your exercise, diet, or stress management plans. You might need to practice a healthier set of attitudes, or you might need to spend more time with people who love you. Tuning up Layers One and Two may be all you'll need to reengage your flow of healing.

If you have thoroughly reviewed and empowered the first two layers of your healing plan and you still feel distressed and stuck, restoring your flow of healing with medicine may be your next step.

The answer to "When is the right time to take medicine?" depends on how much your suffering is blocking your healing process. Manageable distress can sharpen and accelerate the flow of healing and the acquisition of wisdom. Excessive suffering can delay or block healing because it is so distracting.

Medicine for soft psychiatric conditions is one of the most controversial areas of mind healing. Some say it does more harm than good and has no place in problems caused by adversity and trauma. They say psychiatric medicine has no place in helping the mind to heal. Others say medicine does not interfere with healing and can help it. I say psychiatric medicine should only be used for soft anxiety and depression when it assists the flow of healing.

No one should needlessly suffer from anxiety and depression. The goal of a properly constructed healing plan is to permanently cure anxiety or depression without medication when possible and to use medication to reduce symptoms when needed.

Healing Titration

Let's say your efforts to use enhancements and guidance are getting you nowhere and you've decided to try a medicine to see if it will help. Finding the proper dosage can be just as important as determining the proper medicine. Titration is often required to find the proper dose of a medicine that will provide the proper amount of relief. *Titration* is a chemical term that means finding the right spot between too much and too little.

Assuming you have the correct medicine, finding the right dosage for soft anxiety and depression is simple: too much causes blunting and other side effects, and too little has little or no effect. The correct amount of a medicine varies according to the severity of your symptoms and how your body works with the medication. If you familiarize yourself with the most common or most likely side effects, you will be more likely to notice them and use them as a sign that your dose may be too high. The right amount of medicine for you may not be the same as for someone else. The right amount depends mostly on how well it is absorbed and how fast your body metabolizes it—that is, breaks it down. The speed and efficiency of your liver, not the size of your body, more often determine how quickly you metabolize medication. Sometimes a 100-pound person needs twice the dose of someone who weighs 300 pounds.

Genetic tests can determine whether you are a slow or rapid metabolizer of medicine. Your liver has a complex set of enzymes that tear apart molecules so that they can be better used or more easily excreted: Testing can determine the activity levels of your enzymes. These are easy-to-administer blood or saliva tests, and they can help your prescriber determine the dosage of medicine that's right for you.

Finding your proper dosage is still easy enough without genetic testing. Most prescribers start with a low dose of the medicine they hope
will help, and then slowly raise the dosage. If the medicine is going
to work, the most optimal dose can usually be found this way. When
you have gone too high, you will start having unwanted effects like
blunted thoughts and feelings or distressing physical symptoms like
constipation or diarrhea, or sexual side effects. Reduce the dose until
you find the sweet spot with the desired effect and minimal undesired
effects.

Sometimes, though, medicine that works still has undesired side
effects that can't be avoided. That's when you'll have to decide whether
to continue the medicine. Does the benefit of the desired effect out-
weigh the detriment of the undesired effects? If you are able to work
and love, you might be willing to put up with some constipation,
diarrhea, or a sluggish sex drive.

If you are troubled by sexual side effects, such as low sex drive,
sluggish arousal, or lack of orgasm, you may be facing a tough decision. Aside from your own lack of pleasure, sexual side effects can take
a toll on a relationship. If you are in a romantic relationship and your
partner feels unloved or abandoned, then you may need to consider
a different medicine or have a conversation about sexual side effects.

If you take a medicine and it works well with no or few undesired effects, then you have experienced a good outcome. Roughly
one-third of people who take a medicine for distress enjoy virtually
complete resolution ("remission") of symptoms without significant
side effects and without blunting their thoughts or feelings. Another
one-third of medicine users experience a partial positive response.
If you have reduced your distress by at least 50 percent, you are in
that category. With a partial positive effect, you might be on the right

track, but using a similar medicine or adding another medicine might work better. If you are in the unlucky third who realize no effect from a medicine, it may mean you'll need to try a different type of medicine or an additional type of nonmedication therapy such as an additional type of psychotherapy.

Consult with trained professionals before you make a decision about whether to take medicine, what to take, and at what dosage. To help you with a conversation you may have with a prescriber, here's an overview of some medicines that have been found helpful for soft anxiety and depression.

Herbal Remedies

My interest in herbal remedies was sparked by my grandmother's passion for them. Clara Dora Tilly Christiansen Wanck was an herbalist. All it took was a sniffle, a cough, or a bellyache and out came the herbs. Grandma would put me to bed with a mustard pack on my chest or sit me down with a towel over my head and suffuse my face with a steaming pot of herbs.

Grandma was simply continuing the tradition of herbal medicine that she was taught as a child. Herbs were the first medicines, and they still play an important role in many healing plans. Used wisely and carefully, they can work as well as industrial pharmaceuticals. They can also cause side effects and dangerous interactions with other medicines. Just because they are natural doesn't mean they can't hurt you. Arsenic, for example, is natural but you wouldn't want it in your healing plan.

Herbal remedies, like manufactured medicines, can lower the intrusive symptoms of depression and anxiety enough to restore your flow of healing. As with other medicines, they can help you make better use of enhancement and guidance methods to assist your mind in healing.

Medicines derived from herbs provide important information to chemists in labs who seek to develop newer and better pharmaceuticals. Scientists continue to make trips to the Amazon rain forest, where the immense diversity of life forms has produced a vast array of plants with remarkable healing properties. Some people call the Amazon Basin "nature's pharmacy."

Herbal medicines appeal to some because they come directly from living organisms and can be purchased (or grown) without a prescription. Some herbal medicines have been proven effective, but they must be used wisely and cautiously. *Because herbal medicines have pharmacological properties, side effects and drug interactions can occur. It is important to be knowledgeable of these risks and to discuss them with your prescriber or herbalist.*

You should have realistic expectations for the effectiveness of herbal medicines. They can be very helpful for mild to moderate conditions. They have not been shown to work well, however, for severe depression or severe panic.

Herbs for Depression

Scientific studies have shown some herbs, when properly dosed, can relieve depression. They can even rival the effects of manufactured pharmaceutical antidepressants.

St. John's Wort

Though indigenous to Europe, St. John's Wort (*Hyperium perforatum*) is an invasive species in the United States. A yellow flowering perennial, it grows up to three feet tall. The "common" or "perforate" species has translucent dots in its leaves. They are small oil glands that look like little windows when you hold the leaves up to the light. The active ingredients in St. John's Wort, hypericin and hyperforin, are responsible for its antidepressant effect. It typically flowers early in summer and was historically harvested on June 24, St. John's Day. "Wort" means "plant" in Old English.

St. John's Wort, like most antidepressants, works by inhibiting the reuptake of chemicals in your brain called neurotransmitters. This allows greater availability of the neurotransmitters known as serotonin, norepinephrine, and dopamine. These chemicals prevent depression. St. John's Wort also works as a monoamine oxidase inhibitor (MAOI). In this way, it interferes with the elimination of neurotransmitters so that more remain available. As an MAOI, however, high doses of St. John's Wort can cause blood pressure elevation, especially when combined with foods rich in the amino acid tyramine. Tyramine-rich foods include aged cheeses, red wine, fava beans, miso soup, pickled fish, dried meats, and salami. St. John's Wort, especially when combined with other antidepressants (fluoxetine [Prozac], for example) can cause a dangerous condition called serotonin syndrome, which is characterized by high fever, agitation, confusion, and irregular heartbeat.[93] Because of this, St. John's Wort should not be taken with most prescription antidepressants. The combination can be dangerous.

When taken safely, St. John's Wort has been shown to be effective for depression in many scientific tests. An analysis of thirty-seven studies showed that it worked better than a placebo and as well as numerous standard antidepressants.[94] The dose used in most scientific studies is 300 milligrams taken three times daily. Because it is not under the control of the U.S. Food and Drug Administration (FDA), the quality and concentration of St. John's Wort in the United States can vary from one manufacturer to the next. Follow the manufacturer's recommendations along with discussing the proper dosage with your prescriber or herbalist.

Although it may be a pretty flower in your backyard, remember that St. John's Wort can have potent effects on your body, including side effects and drug interactions. Investigate it and discuss it as thoroughly as you would a prescription antidepressant.[95]

Saffron

Another flower, saffron (*Crocus sativus*) has been shown to have antidepressant effects.[96] The saffron crocus is a perennial. The three threadlike stigmas in each flower are painstakingly plucked and dried. Because it is so labor intensive to produce, saffron is the most expensive spice in the world.[97]

Fortunately, not much is needed. Thirty milligrams, the usual amount used in cooking, was the dose studied in several trials.[98] In one trial it was compared to a standard dose (20 milligrams per day) of Prozac (fluoxetine). In another, it was compared to a standard dose of 100 milligrams per day of imipramine (an older, tricyclic antidepressant). In both cases, saffron was found to be just as effective and safe up to a dose of 5 grams.[99] At higher doses, however, its anticoagulant effects could be dangerous, especially if you already take a blood thinner like Coumadin. You need to let your medical doctor know if you choose to take saffron.

Turmeric

Popular in Indian cooking, turmeric may also have antidepressant effects. Its active agent, curcumin, has been found to enhance the effectiveness of several antidepressants.[100] Turmeric has also been shown to be more effective than a placebo, especially in people who sleep and eat excessively when they are depressed.[101] In a study comparing curcumin and Prozac (fluoxetine) over a six-week period for sixty people with major depression, some were given 20 milligrams of Prozac (a standard dose), some were given 1000 milligrams of curcumin, and some were given both.[102] The curcumin group did just as well as the Prozac group, and the people who took both fared even better. Although further research is needed to replicate the claims for saffron and turmeric, you might cautiously include these spices in your diet, especially if you like their taste.

Herbs for Anxiety

Several herbal remedies for anxiety have been proven better than a placebo and as good as antianxiety pharmaceuticals. You might have already used one of them in tea to calm yourself in the evening.

Chamomile

Chamomile (*Matricaria recutita*) is a member of the daisy family that grows in the wild in temperate climates. It looks like a daisy and smells like an apple. Chamomile's dried flowers are used in tea and contain a variety of active ingredients, including apigenin. Apigenin binds to benzodiazepine receptors in the human brain, which allows it to work like Valium (diazepam), Xanax (alprazolam), and other medications in the benzodiazepine class of manufactured pharmaceuticals. In tests for its antianxiety properties, when chamomile was compared to placebo, it showed a significant reduction of anxiety with very few side effects.[103] In the study, the researchers used pharmaceutical-grade German chamomile with 1.2 percent apigenin in 200-milligram capsules with the number of capsules gradually increased to a maximum of five per day. While a cup of chamomile tea does not have as much active ingredient as was used in the study, these results may explain how chamomile tea might help calm your nerves.

Kava–Kava

Also known as kava, this herb has been the subject of numerous scientific studies. In a twenty-five-week trial, kava-kava was compared to a placebo and found to be significantly effective in reducing anxiety.[104] In other studies, kava was found to be as effective as antidepressants and benzodiazepines for mild to moderate anxiety.[105]

Caution should be exercised with kava as with any other herb. Kava can cause liver toxicity and skin lesions, especially if taken at high doses.

Passionflower

An anxiety-relieving herb found in temperate climates is passionflower (*Passiflora incarnate*). It is indigenous to North America, where its leaves had been used medicinally long before European colonialists arrived. In 1978 the FDA prohibited its use in over-the-counter preparations because it had not been proven safe and effective, despite centuries of use by Native Americans.

A recent study may help reverse the FDA's position. In the study, passionflower was compared to oxazepam, a benzodiazepine like Valium or Xanax. Passionflower was found to have just as much anti-anxiety effect as the prescription medicine; oxazepam, however, caused impairment in job performance whereas passionflower did not.[106]

Valerian

Valerian (*Valeriana officinalis*) is frequently used to reduce anxiety and to produce mild sedation to help sleep.[107] It is a perennial flowering plant native to Europe and Asia and introduced to North America. It appears to work by binding GABA (a naturally calming brain chemical), benzodiazepine, and barbiturate receptors.[108] As a result, it works like benzodiazepines such as Valium and Xanax.[109] Withdrawal symptoms have been reported upon suddenly stopping substantial doses of valerian.[110] Don't exceed the manufacturer's recommended dose limit unless a prescriber or herbalist suggests it.

As with standard pharmaceuticals, herbal medicines can also blunt your feelings and interfere with healing and growth—and as with standard pharmaceuticals, herbal medicines should only be used in the service of healing. Titration of dosages between too little effect and too much effect is necessary, and if and when herbal medicines seem to be of negligible help, or if they interfere with the flow of your healing by blunting your thoughts and feelings, they should be carefully tapered and discontinued. As always, consult with a person knowledgeable about herbal medicines and their possible interactions with manufactured pharmaceuticals.

Nonverbal Herbal Communication

The relationship between herbs and humans is old and mysterious. For millennia, humans and other species have benefited from the healing effects of herbs. Sometimes herbal healing benefits are discovered in interesting and mysterious ways.

When I accompanied my grandmother as she foraged for herbs, I was amazed by how easily she could find them. On one of our treks, my grandmother stopped in a clearing. She stood still, closed her eyes, and slowed her breathing. After she opened her eyes, she walked directly to the species of herb she was seeking. She told me they talked to her. Given her earthy and spiritual ways, I was not surprised. For me, our walks were magical adventures. For Grandma, they were trips to nature's pharmacy.

Years later I traveled by dugout canoe to an isolated tribe in the Peruvian Amazon. I'd hoped to study with a shaman. My acceptance by the shaman was contingent on my response to the effect of an herb I was required to ingest. As I sat in a circle of men sharing a green, frothy liquid from a hand-carved wooden bowl, I wondered if I had made a rational decision. Fortunately, when I shared my enjoyment of watching colorful fish leap from the ground and of breathing in rhythm with the trees, I was accepted. The hallucinogenic herb was from the bark of the root of a bush. It was prepared by women who chewed the bark and spit into a bowl. Their saliva activated the herb by releasing the psychoactive alkaloids from the bark. Basically, we drank their spit. When I asked how they knew where to find this substance and how to prepare it, I was told, "This has always been known."

More recently, my old, blind dog had a stroke and could not eat, drink, or walk on his own. He was not in pain or distress, was aware of his surroundings, and seemed happy to be carried and petted. I tried nursing him back to health by squirting water and food into his mouth with a syringe. Then I took him outside for some fresh air.

When I sat him on the lawn (which is chemical free), he began voraciously eating a plant called Creeping Charlie. *Glechoma hederacea* (Creeping Charlie's scientific name) is a member of the mint family known to have medicinal effects. Not long after his self-administered dose of Creeping Charlie, my dog began walking and drinking on his own. What I found most interesting is that a dog who previously could not eat or drink would select that specific plant among others within his reach and eat it with gusto. Maybe it's a coincidence that my dog's symptoms improved after eating Creeping Charlie, but I'm now happy to add it to my salads!

Grandma, my shaman, and my dog share the experience of being drawn to specific herbs for specific reasons. Is there an unspoken awareness that some humans (and dogs) have of the healing powers of herbs? Perhaps we are linked to herbs in ways science can't describe.

Light Therapy for Seasonal Affective Disorder

Seasonal affective disorder (SAD), also known as the "winter blues," is a type of depression that's usually easy to fix. It affects approximately 10 percent of the people who live in temperate and cold climates approximately thirty-nine degrees latitude north or south of the equator.[111, 112] In the northern hemisphere SAD most often occurs north of Washington, D.C., and it can happen to people who have had no significant adversity in their lives. If you live or visit north of Washington, D.C., more than one month in the winter and if you have seasonal affective disorder, you may become depressed and have less energy during winter months.

What most people don't realize is that seasonal affective disorder is not an illness; it's a brilliant vestigial evolutionary adaptation that some of us still share with other mammals like bears, rabbits, squirrels, and chipmunks.* Although some people call slowing down in the winter "hibernation," it's technically a form of mild dormancy. It's not the deep sleep of near death that reptiles, amphibians, and insects can manage when they experience true hibernation. It's a pattern of behavior that involves slowing down and sleeping more. Its adaptive function for early humans was to conserve food supplies during long winter months.

Sometimes people who live away from the equator don't know they have seasonal affective disorder because it mimics clinical depression. SAD shares many of the symptoms of clinical depression—low energy, sadness, lack of interest, and absence of pleasure—is often incorrectly diagnosed as depression, and is often unnecessarily treated with antidepressant pharmaceuticals. If you have SAD, using light therapy (phototherapy) may be all you need. SAD responds well to full-spectrum light therapy without the side effects of pharmaceutical medicines.[113]

Just because SAD often responds to full-spectrum light doesn't mean it's a mild problem. In addition to feeling depressed, those who have SAD can believe they are lazy and lack ambition. Having less energy, they become easily overwhelmed by the struggle to maintain their usual level of productivity. Jobs and relationships can be threatened by the effects of seasonal affective disorder. Sometimes

---

* Actually, SAD only affects omnivores. Rabbits, squirrels, and chipmunks include in their diet insects, which are technically animals, and squirrels occasionally eat eggs and young birds (yikes!) if they can't find enough nuts. Strict herbivores, like deer, do not "hibernate," nor do carnivores like fox, coyotes, and wildcats. Domestic dogs have evolved into omnivores, but they, like most of us humans, have lost the SAD gene.

otherwise bright and capable children who have SAD need to repeat a year of school.

If you live far from the equator and have seasonal affective disorder, you don't have to move closer to the equator, and you don't have to take an antidepressant. Most people with SAD experience full relief of symptoms when they use light therapy. There are two types of light therapy units: full spectrum and blue. Since blue is the predominant wave length that inhibits melatonin release, using a unit that casts a blue light may be sufficient. The benefit is that the blue light is smaller, lighter, and less expensive than most full-spectrum units. There's also less eyestrain; full-spectrum light is harsh. The disadvantage with the blue wave length is that it may not be sufficient. Some people have told me that the blue wave length units they've tried are not as effective as full-spectrum.

The usual procedure is to set the unit twenty inches from your face and sit in front of it for thirty minutes every morning. It's not necessary to look directly at the light. As long as the light enters your eye indirectly, you'll have the desired effect. Most people have breakfast or read in front of it. It's important to use it in the morning so that it doesn't keep you awake at night.

A cautionary note about exposure to light at night: Don't read a mobile electronic device before sleep unless you place an amber filter over it. Most portable electronic devices emit blue light, which can wake you up just like a phototherapy unit. The light from your device (cell phone, tablet, computer) can suppress the release of melatonin and keep you from falling asleep easily. Amber filters block blue light while allowing the other wavelengths to pass through. Most portable electronic devices are equipped with a setting that turns the screen amber for bedtime viewing. Some people also use amber sunglasses to be sure they block out the blue light so they can sleep. I'm told they're quite a sight in bed!

Manufactured Pharmaceuticals

Psychiatric pharmaceutical medicines are crude. They affect organs other than the brain, and they affect the brain in more ways than intended. Most criticism of psychiatric medication focuses on how bad it can be for you to take it. Some criticism is focused on how poorly it works.

I struggle with mixed feelings about prescribing medicine for anxiety and depression. I'm painfully aware of its risks and dangers. Psychiatric medicine can cause troublesome and sometimes serious side effects. It can even cause death. I've also, however, seen it save lives, relationships, and lifestyles.

I still worry about the dangers, though, and I share what I know about them with my patients. Some people tire of my warnings; others appreciate them. I remind my patients that psychiatric pharmaceuticals, though sometimes helpful, can also interfere with the goal of eradication of soft anxiety and depression by other means like counseling and spiritual guidance.

Criticism about how bad psychiatric medicine can be and how poorly it often works is warranted but not always well informed. Most medicines work better for severe conditions than for mild or moderate ones. If you take medicine for a mild condition, it can be hard to know if it's doing any good. Although the medicines we have now are better and safer than earlier versions, they still need to be improved. As someone who has studied and prescribed medicine for decades, I am disappointed by how little we know, grateful for how far we have come, and excited about the discoveries ahead.

The brain is the most complex organ in the body, with somewhere between 50 and 100 billion nerve cells, all interconnected and firing in complicated sequences. How can we possibly understand the brain well enough to give it drugs that are poorly understood and cause effects that are often unpredictable? We have much to learn about how best to help.

Antidepressants

Antidepressants and antianxiety drugs are the psychiatric pharmaceutical medicines most often used. They are also the classes of pharmaceuticals most likely to be offered to you. When they are used for soft anxiety and depression, their limitations may be more obvious than their benefits.

Confusion about the safety of antidepressants abounds for good reason. They have earned the dreaded "black box" warning from the FDA, signifying that medical studies have shown the drug carries a significant risk of causing serious or even life-threatening events. In the case of antidepressants, the Food and Drug Administration (FDA) adopted a "black box" label stating that SSRI antidepressants may increase the risk of suicidal thinking and behavior in some children, adolescents, and young adults with major depressive disorder.[114] But wait! Aren't they supposed to *prevent* suicide?

Many scientific studies have shown that antidepressants save lives by preventing suicide.[115] This seeming conflict between study results arises because an increased risk of suicide is present when someone first starts taking an antidepressant for depression, but the risk diminishes after the antidepressant takes full effect.

Depression has physical as well as emotional and cognitive symptoms. Unless you experience what's known as *agitated depression*, you are likely to slow down when you are depressed. This is called *psychomotor retardation*. Talk show host Dick Cavett once said that when he was depressed, "If [a magic wand] were eight feet away, it would be too impossible a feat to go and get it."[116] A person with psychomotor retardation often lacks the energy to commit suicide. The problem with antidepressants is that they often relieve the symptom of psychomotor retardation before they relieve hopelessness. That is why the risk of suicide can be higher when beginning to take an antidepressant. If you still feel hopeless but have more energy to act on your hopelessness, you are at greater risk for suicide.

Whenever I give people an antidepressant prescription, I also give them a warning. I tell them that when they first start taking the antidepressant, they may have the energy to harm themselves before the wish to do so goes away. I explain that they must not harm themselves—that they must wait for the antidepressant to take full effect. I often give a "safety card" that reads, "You may believe you will never get better, but you will. Misery is temporary even though it may feel permanent." Then I list names and phone numbers of people to call if their depression feels unbearable.

I explain to people before they take an antidepressant that when we humans feel miserable, we often think it will continue forever. I call this the *delusion of permanent misery*. It is a flaw in our nature that natural selection has not yet eliminated and that makes no sense. Why don't we have the delusion that we will be *happy* forever? Why must we believe we will suffer forever when we don't get to believe we will enjoy a state of joy forever? In fact, your feelings of misery, like feelings of joy, will not last. Feelings naturally diminish over time or are replaced by other feelings. We must take steps to protect ourselves from the false belief that misery is permanent. I realize false beliefs don't just go away because I tell them to. I ask people to humor me by staying alive long enough to find out that their misery will pass. I ask them to resist the urge to cause self-harm long enough for the antidepressant to relieve their sadness. If someone cannot promise this in good faith, we talk about what steps to take (going to a hospital or having relatives keep a close watch) to keep them from hurting themselves until the urge to do so passes.

Additional Side Effects of Antidepressants

I am pleasantly surprised when someone receives a desired effect from an antidepressant with no undesired effects. The desired effects are relief of depression and, for some, relief of anxiety. The possible side effects are more numerous.

One of the most frequent and noteworthy side effects of antidepressants is loss of sex drive and function. Depression and anxiety themselves can cause diminished sexual desire and diminished or absent arousal. Erection, lubrication, orgasm, and ejaculation can be impaired by suffering or side effects. Here's how to tell if your trouble with sex is caused by medicine: If you are feeling better, with greater optimism and enjoyment, but you lack interest in sex or if sex doesn't work as well, it could be due to the side effects of medication. If you're feeling better, you may not care (but your partner might).

Antidepressants can cause problems for the second most intelligent organ system in your body—your gastrointestinal (GI) tract. (You have 100 billion nerve cells in your brain, but you also have 100 million nerve cells in your GI tract.) Because the GI tract contains serotonin receptors, serotonin-enhancing antidepressants can cause nausea and diarrhea. Moreover, because the GI tract also has norepinephrine receptors, norepinephrine-enhancing medications can cause constipation and dry mouth.

Some antidepressants can cause blood pressure changes, cardiac arrhythmias (irregular heartbeats), and dangerous interactions with other medicines. Be sure to tell your prescriber what other pharmaceuticals, herbal medicines, and recreational drugs you may be taking so that serious drug interactions can be avoided.

Benzodiazepines

Benzodiazepines, commonly called "benzos," are surprisingly popular given the bad reputation they have earned. They are popular because they rapidly and effectively reduce anxiety. In our stress-filled culture, this is a big selling point. When benzos finish their job of reducing anxiety, they become sedating. This is why many people use them for sleep even though this is not an official indication for most of them.

Fast-acting benzodiazepines can stop a panic attack in its tracks and then stick around for a few hours to help you manage residual anxiety. They can also help prevent or reduce overwhelming anxiety when taken before an especially scary situation. Most often, however, they are used to reduce ongoing daily anxiety and stress. That is when they can interfere with healing.

Anxiety provides urgency and drive to enhance the awareness needed for conflict resolution. The most effective work on resolving childhood adversity and trauma in therapy is fueled by anxiety. Without enough anxiety, unconscious conflicts are not driven into awareness. Too high a dose of a benzodiazepine can reduce anxiety so much that it can interfere with awareness of and resolution of conflict.

If you are taking a benzodiazepine, I suggest you discuss proper dosing with your prescriber and therapist. They may be able to help you find the right dose between healing restoration and healing interference.

When taken at the proper dosage and for the purpose of assisting healing, benzodiazepines can be helpful. They can be dangerous when taken to excess or combined with alcohol or other depressant classes of drugs. Be sure to discuss all of your medical conditions and all of your medicines with your prescriber before you consider taking one.

If you are in recovery from an addiction, taking an antidepressant rather than a benzodiazepine might help reduce the intensity of your anxiety without increasing your risk of relapse and would prevent the risk of becoming addicted to a benzodiazepine. Some antidepressants work as well for anxiety as they do for depression. Many people, in fact, take an antidepressant for anxiety rather than for depression. Keep in mind that, as previously discussed, an antidepressant could blunt your emotions and expose you to side effects.

Side Effects of Benzodiazepines

An important concern about benzodiazepines is that they can be addictive. If you take one at a high dose or for a long time, you could have trouble getting off it. If you have or have had a problem with alcohol, drug use, or addictive behaviors, benzodiazepines could cause a relapse, and they may be more likely to become a new addiction.

Combining benzodiazepines with alcohol, barbiturates, or opiates is dangerous for everyone. When taken in combination, their effects are multiplied rather than added. The magnified effects can cause serious problems with judgment. When taken with alcohol, barbiturates, or opiates, a benzodiazepine can cause you to stop breathing, even when the dosage is small.

If you are struggling to establish or maintain sobriety from alcohol, drug abuse, or an addictive behavior, taking benzodiazepines could throw you off course. Having had an addictive pattern puts you at a higher risk of developing addiction to benzodiazepines. Taking them can also shift your focus from what you need to do to stay sober.

When Soft Becomes Hardened

Soft anxiety and depression can become hardened and cause actual biological changes when abuse or neglect is severe or repetitive and persistent. Severe adversity can create changes in the brain that cannot be easily reprogrammed. Persistent abuse patterns can result in observable changes in gene expression and brain function. Anxiety and depression can become anatomically hardwired.

This has been observed in mouse pups that did not receive enough licking from their mothers. The abuse was in the form of persistent neglect. The wrong genes were switched on, and those pups developed differently than pups that benefited from enough attention.[117] The neglected pups became listless and sickly. Because the neglect was prolonged, their persistent fear and disappointment became hardened into observable physical characteristics: The changes in the structure and function of their brains and ways in which their genes were activated could be measured in the lab. The good news is that this effect was reversible. When the neglected pups were later given enough attention, their symptoms reduced and their genes and brains changed for the better.[118]

The same effect has been discovered in humans. Childhood adversity can cause changes in your genes and changes in your brain. The effect of childhood abuse was studied by a group headed by P. O.

McGowan and reported in the journal *Natural Neuroscience* in 2009. The group did autopsies of people who died by suicide, comparing those who had been subjected to abuse in childhood to those who were not. They also autopsied controls (people who died from causes other than suicide with no history of childhood abuse). They found measurable differences in the genes and the brains of people who were abused in childhood.[119]

Genetic changes were responsible for changes in the hippocampal brain activity of the studied subjects. (The hippocampus is the part of your brain responsible for feelings and memories.) The genetic effect was the same for abused human children as for neglected mouse pups. The researchers showed how persistent adversity can have an effect on gene expression and how disordered gene expression causes changes in the brains of humans. Their study clearly demonstrates how childhood adversity can become biologically hardened to cause persistent suffering.

Can Childhood Adversity Cause a Permanent Problem?

Early life adversity does not necessarily cause permanent change, but a lot of work may be needed to reverse the effects of persistent adversity. As the McGowan study suggests, even biological hardening may be reversible with the proper interventions. Medicine may be needed to reduce symptoms enough to restore healing so that psychotherapy or spiritual guidance and healing enhancements can do their work. Then with time and hard work, healing may reverse even detectable physical changes by changing the epigenetic mechanisms that caused the changes in the first place.

Even when severe or persistent adversity becomes physically detectable, it can respond to healing. When adversity causes symptoms of anxiety and depression severe enough to delay or derail healing, medicine may reduce symptoms enough to restore the flow of healing. When healing is restored, enhancement and guidance have a better chance of resulting in a cure.

Herbal Medicines for Soft Psychiatric Conditions

Herbal medicines may be helpful if too much sadness or fear blocks your capacity to heal with enhancement and guidance alone.

For persistent severe sadness

- St. John's Wort (can be dangerous if combined with pharmaceutical antidepressants)
- Saffron
- Turmeric

For persistent severe anxiety

- Chamomile
- Kava-Kava (caution: may cause liver toxicity)
- Passionflower
- Valerian

Use only as directed by a qualified herbalist or prescriber.

Pharmaceutical Medicines for
Soft Psychiatric Conditions

These medications may be helpful if too much sadness or anxiety blocks your capacity to heal with enhancement and guidance alone.

For persistent severe sadness

Antidepressants: Can make severe sadness more manageable.

- Could take several weeks before they work
- Watch for side effects and brain blunting (dulling of feelings and mental sharpness)

For persistent severe anxiety

Antidepressants: Some can help reduce anxiety.

- May take several weeks to work
- Watch for side effects and brain blunting

Benzodiazepines: Can rapidly reduce anxiety.

- Strong addiction potential
- Safe with antidepressants but can be dangerous if taken with alcohol, barbiturates, or opiates
- Brain blunting can slow healing
- Use only as directed by a qualified prescriber; using too much can hurt you

CHAPTER 12

Medicine for Hard Anxiety and Depression

You can't just talk your way out of some conditions.

*I*f you are not getting better despite the steps I've recommended so far, you might have hard instead of soft anxiety or depression. Hard anxiety and depression are more biological than psychological. "Hard" means that the condition is hardwired rather than programmed and that it is unlikely to be resolved without medicine. Hard anxiety or depression may have been transmitted to you genetically, or it may be the result of severe and persistent adversity or trauma that became so ingrained that the symptoms may not be alleviated without medicine.

233

"Hard" is not an official diagnosis. It's a concept I developed to help me know when my patients may need medicine—that they may not get well without it. The difference between soft and hard anxiety or depression is that medicine may be helpful for soft but that it may be necessary for hard.

The concept of hard anxiety and depression is practical and useful, and many scientific studies support the notion that some types of anxiety and depression are more physical than psychological and need the power of medicine for a reasonable outcome. Hard conditions are generally thought to be medical conditions. Even health insurance companies view conditions like major depression, bipolar disorder, and panic disorder this way. Their expectation is that treatment with medicine will likely be necessary.

My patients have found hard anxiety and depression a useful concept. They tell me it helps to know that medicine might provide the relief they seek if their anxiety or depression is unresponsive to therapy, spiritual guidance, and healthy behaviors. Knowing that their condition may be "hard" lifts some of the pressure they sometimes feel to solve their problems without medicine, and knowing there could be a biological reason for their distress helps relieve the guilt they may feel about taking medicine.

Causes of Hard Anxiety and Depression

The two primary causes of hard anxiety and depression are genetics and severe or persistent adversity or trauma. It's possible to have one cause without the other, and both causes can coexist. Remember that symptoms of anxiety or depression can also result from an underlying medical condition or addiction. As I explained in chapter

3, medical conditions and addiction can mimic the primary causes of anxiety and depression.*

Persistent, Severe Adversity or Trauma

Persistent adversity due to trauma or stress can, if not relieved, result in a hardened condition that does not respond well to therapy alone. Some people who are subjected to persistent adversity develop hardened anxiety or depression even when little or no family history would suggest a genetic cause of their distress. In those cases, severe persistent adversity causes a wound so deep that the resulting anxiety or depression does not resolve easily without the use of medicine. Just as repetitive use of an injured joint can cause a serious orthopedic problem, so can repetitive abuse of a psyche. Just as persistent stress can cause acid reflux that may become difficult to resolve, so can repetitive abuse cause erosion of self-esteem deep enough for the resulting depression to become resistant to treatment without medicine. The effects of repetitive, severe adversity may eventually be eased by persistent loving-kindness, healthy behaviors, a strong spiritual practice, and long-term talk therapy, but medicine may be needed to reduce the symptoms of depression enough for loving-kindness and therapeutic guidance to wear away the scarring caused by persistent adversity.

Studies have shown that severe or persistent childhood adversity can set the stage for deeper wounds in adulthood.[120, 121] When substantial adversity—such as physical or sexual abuse, unrelenting criticism, or neglect—is suffered in childhood, traumatic adulthood events like

---

* Primary causes are unreasonable stress, childhood adversity or trauma, and genetics. An underactive thyroid gland can mimic depression; so can too much alcohol. If hard anxiety or depression is not caused by a medical problem or an addiction, then it is being caused by genetics or severe adversity, or a combination of the two.

combat, rape, assault, or persistent bullying can cause more pain than if they were preceded by a safe and nurturing childhood. If you experienced significant adversity as a child, be aware that you could be more vulnerable to adulthood trauma than if you'd had a safer and more nurturing childhood.

When someone's depression or anxiety appears to have been hardened by severe adversity, I never give up on the possible resolution of distress with Layer One: Enhancement and Layer Two: Guidance, even while someone's depression or anxiety is being treated with medicine. A case of hard anxiety or depression can often be gradually dissolved with the persistent application of healing-assisting actions. Sometimes enough healing can allow medication to be tapered and even discontinued.

If you think you may have hard anxiety or depression and decide to use medicine, I urge you to continue to use Layers One and Two to enhance and guide your healing while you are taking medicine. Continuing healing enhancement and guidance will help you

- Stay fit and physically healthy by practicing health-promoting behaviors.
- Address the challenges of coping with residual symptoms of anxiety or depression that medicine may not fully relieve.
- Manage and resolve distress caused by relationship problems so that the source of stress does not worsen your condition.
- Reduce the severity of hard anxiety and depression with psychotherapy and other nonmedicinal approaches, which may then allow a reduction of dosage of medicine.

I have seen people with soft anxiety or depression decide too quickly to take medicine, thereby robbing themselves of the chance for a cure with psychotherapy and other nonmedicinal approaches. However, I have also seen people with hard anxiety or depression suffer needlessly in their struggle for resolution of distress without the help of medicine. Just as some people give up on therapy and turn to medicine too soon, others struggle and suffer needlessly to resolve hard anxiety or a hard depressive condition without medicine. We remain limited in our ability to diagnose hard or hardened anxiety or depression. Reliable, accurate, and affordable testing for the diagnosis of genetic anxiety and depression is on the horizon but not yet available. Laboratory testing and imaging studies still cannot determine with certainty that someone has suffered neurological changes caused by relationship adversity. However, some exciting scientific findings substantiate the concept of hard anxiety and depression and point to the future development of laboratory and imaging studies to help us know when someone has hard rather than soft anxiety or depression. Since most of the findings regarding hard conditions involve genetic depression, I'll start there.

Genetics

Genetic inheritance is considered by clinicians and scientists to be the cause of many cases of hardwired anxiety or depression. If your biological parents or grandparents had severe anxiety or depression, then you might have inherited it. This is why most clinicians ask if there's a family history of anxiety or depression. If it's likely that you inherited anxiety or depression, it's a good idea to educate yourself about it. The more you know, the more you can do to help yourself. If you have children or other relatives with anxiety or depression, you can show them how to deal with it.

Researchers are striving to identify the specific genes implicated in some types of hard anxiety and depression. They are discovering that for many types of hard anxiety and depression, multiple genes may be involved, and whether those genes are expressed or not depends largely on environmental factors like stress and trauma. The field of study called *epigenetics* bridges the gap between genetics and environment by showing how unhealthy factors like stress and trauma can switch on unwanted genes and how healthy factors like exercise and a good diet can switch them off. In addition to identifying the genes involved in anxiety and depression, researchers are discovering the specific epigenetic factors that turn those genes on and off and how they do it.

Depression Caused by Genetic Factors

As with many conditions, depression can run in families. Sometimes depression is transmitted by learning and modeling: If your mother or father viewed life negatively, you may have learned to do the same. That's an example of soft depression. When depression is embedded in your DNA, it is a hardwired problem.

Genetics can play such an important role in depression that I always ask my depressed patients if any of their blood relatives or ancestors have or have had depression. If the response is yes, I ask if anything has helped. If a treatment has helped a genetic relative, it may help my patient.

This is an exciting time for research in genetic depression. The Psychiatric Genomics Consortium, a major player in the field of genetic depression research, has more than eight hundred scientists from thirty-eight countries analyzing data from more than 1 million patients. Their findings about genetic depression are exciting and encouraging.

The genetics of serotonin deficient depression has been extensively studied with interesting results.[122, 123, 124] Scientists have found that a particular version of a gene affecting serotonin called the S-allele version of the serotonin transporter appears to be a *plasticity gene*.[125, 126] This means the gene is more likely to be activated if the person with the gene experienced childhood adversity. If someone's childhood environment was safe and nurturing, the gene is less likely to be activated and cause depression.[127] It was even found that, with this gene, those who experienced more severe childhood adversity suffered more severe depression (based upon the number of suicide attempts made).

Although some argue that genetics plays no role at all—believing that the depression that researchers described was entirely due to childhood adversity,[128] many studies suggest genetics plays a prominent role, accounting for 50 percent of the cause of serious ("major") depression.[129] Given the variable responses depressed people have to serotonin-enhancing medicines, it is possible that gene and environment interactions (called gene x environment) are more important for serotonin-deficient depression than for norepinephrine-deficient depression.

Scientists are discovering that norepinephrine-deficient depression may have a stronger genetic link than serotonin-deficient depression. I have several patients who enjoy complete resolution of their depression when they take norepinephrine-enhancing medication. They have no significant childhood adversity and no current relationship distress, so there's not much evidence of adversity and not much need for therapy. I tell them their depression seems to be more in their brain than in their mind. There are research findings that support the notion that norepinephrine-deficient depression may be less plastic, meaning less influenced by the environment than serotonin-deficient depression.[130]

Researchers have claimed that they successfully matched a specific gene that causes norepinephrine-deficient depression with an antidepressant that treats the depression caused by that gene.[131] They reported that their patient's symptoms significantly resolved when they took the pharmaceutical medicine venlafaxine (brand name Effexor). Venlafaxine helps make more norepinephrine available where it's needed to reverse the symptoms of depression. By using genetic typing (called *genotyping*), researchers identified a group of people with the gene thought to be causing their norepinephrine-deficient depression. The group with the gene affecting their norepinephrine, in fact, responded remarkably well when they were given therapeutic doses of venlafaxine. The researchers hope this may lead to the development of a blood or saliva test that will successfully determine who will benefit from venlafaxine. This research may lead to the development of a reliable and affordable test for a specific type of depression that may be relieved by a specific medicine.

Genetic Panic

Scientific studies have shown that some cases of panic disorder are likely due to genetics. Genetic panic is characterized by panic attacks that come out of the blue and have nothing to do with stressful circumstances. If panic attacks are unrelated to stress, medical conditions, or drug use, they may be caused by genetics.[132]

It is possible for panic to be caused by both genetics and stressful circumstances. When genetic panic is combined with childhood adversity or adulthood stress, panic attacks may be severe, persistent, and distracting. If they do not respond to guidance, treating them with medicine may help. Some benzodiazepines have an immediate effect. They can decrease the intensity and frequency of panic attacks and lower the amount of ongoing anxiety you experience. They can also blunt feelings and slow thinking. They can slow the process of healing if they are taken at too high a dose. They can also cause addiction if taken for a long time at a high dose. If you are taking a benzodiazepine, take as little as possible so that you are less likely to become addicted.

Some antidepressants can help prevent panic attacks. Although they may be helpful, they can cause emotional blunting, gastrointestinal side effects and drug interactions, and suppress sex drive and functioning. They should only be used to reduce the symptoms of panic when those symptoms are so severe they do not respond to the approaches of Layers One and Two.

Pharmaceutical Medicine for Hard Depression

While the information that follows is accurate as of this writing, continuing advances in the field of neuroscience may already have made some of my comments about pharmaceuticals outdated by the time you read this. Be sure to discuss the latest advances in pharmaceutical treatment with your prescriber, therapist, and pharmacist, as well as the possible dangers of taking a pharmaceutical. Just because a medicine is new doesn't mean it is safe.

Most of the antidepressant medications currently on the market increase either serotonin or norepinephrine, the neurotransmitters discussed in the section about genetic depression. Someone's response to an antidepressant can help determine whether their depression is primarily due to serotonin or norepinephrine deficiency. Be sure you're aware of the possible side effects and drug interactions of a pharmaceutical before you decide to take one.

Waiting to see if an antidepressant will work can be tedious. Because a series of biochemical reactions in brain cells must happen before an antidepressant will take effect, it can take several weeks to know if the antidepressant will help. It's also not unusual for undesired side effects to show up before the true antidepressant effect occurs. That's when you may need to decide whether to tolerate side effects while waiting to see if a positive worthwhile effect will be achieved. Sometimes it's necessary to try more than one antidepressant in order to find one that works.

Augmentation of Antidepressants

After trying several antidepressants, if none is sufficiently effective, several add-on pharmaceuticals exist that might help achieve the desired effect. Adding one medicine to another to try for a better effect is called *augmentation*. The hope is that the medicine added to an antidepressant will augment, or strengthen, the effect of the antidepressant.

Adding another medicine can sometimes result in complete resolution of the symptoms of depression. Two medicines used as augmenters of antidepressants are lithium and an atypical antipsychotic medicine called aripiprazole (brand name Abilify).

Atypical antipsychotic medication is a poorly named category because the medicines in this group have effects other than reducing psychotic symptoms. Aripiprazole has FDA approval to be used in combination with an antidepressant for treatment of major depressive disorder when an antidepressant used alone does not give an adequate response to antidepressants.[133] Sometimes adding aripiprazole results in an improved antidepressant effect.[134]

Depression can partially be caused by a deficiency of dopamine, the reward or pleasure neurotransmitter, and aripiprazole appears to help depression because of its effect on dopamine. By moderating the amount of dopamine in the brain, aripiprazole can stabilize mood fluctuation and counteract depression.

Lithium is a trace mineral that, like sodium, can be found virtually anywhere on the planet. There have been reports that communities having a higher than usual concentration of lithium in their drinking water have a lower than usual incidence of depression, suicide, and crime.[135] Although it has long been the gold standard for the treatment of mania, lithium has often been used in low doses to enhance the effectiveness of antidepressants. Lithium appears to have the added benefit of reducing the risk of suicide as reported in several studies.[136] It can, however, cause damage to the kidneys and the thyroid gland. The function of these organs should be closely followed with blood tests if you take lithium.

Bipolar Depression Cautionary Note

Bipolar depression is the depression phase of bipolar disorder (which in the past was called manic depression). Considerable anxiety and depression can be associated with bipolar disorder, for which medicine may be helpful. The genetics of bipolar disorder is still being researched. According to a very large study, there may be overlap between the genetics of bipolar disorder and that of schizophrenia as well as depression,[137] which means that if someone in your genetic background had schizophrenia or a significant case of depression, you might have a greater chance of developing bipolar disorder through genetic inheritance.

Some people become profoundly depressed during the depressive phase of bipolar disorder. This can be a dangerous time because hopelessness and suicide risk can be high.[138] In carefully selected cases, an antidepressant is sometimes added. This move can be risky because an antidepressant can trigger a manic episode in someone who has bipolar disorder. It is necessary to take a mania-preventing medication (a mood stabilizer) any time an antidepressant is taken for bipolar disorder. Even with the protection of a mood stabilizer, however, a manic episode could still erupt if an antidepressant were taken for a depressive phase of bipolar disorder. If you know you have (or if you think you might have) bipolar disorder, I recommend you see someone who has training and experience in the diagnosis and treatment of bipolar disorder to advise you about the use of pharmaceuticals.

Genetic Testing for Antidepressants

Although we don't yet have accurate, reliable, and affordable gene testing to tell what kind of depression you have, or specifically which antidepressant medicine will help, we do have gene testing that will show how rapidly you metabolize antidepressants (as well as other drugs).[139] This can be very useful because people metabolize antidepressants at varying speeds.[140] If you metabolize a medicine more rapidly than expected, you may need a higher dose than expected to get the desired blood level and therapeutic effect. Conversely, if you metabolize a medication slowly, a typical dose could be toxic due to an excessively high blood level.

How rapidly you metabolize an antidepressant can also be affected by the other medicines or herbal remedies you take or the food you eat. Some medicines can inhibit the enzymes that metabolize other medicines. For example, if you take fluoxetine (Prozac) and amitriptyline (an older but effective antidepressant with potentially dangerous cardiac side effects), the fluoxetine can suppress the enzymes that metabolize amitriptyline, placing you at risk of a cardiac arrhythmia and death. If you slowly metabolize venlafaxine because of your genetics and if you consume a lot of grapefruit, the naringen in the grapefruit could inhibit the enzyme that metabolizes venlafaxine and a dangerous toxic blood level of venlafaxine could result.

Knowing whether your enzymes function rapidly or slowly can give you important and protective information. I discovered by genetic testing that one of my patients was a rapid metabolizer; he shared the information with his anesthesiologist and requested a high enough dose of anesthetic so he would not awaken during surgery. It worked, but he woke up just as he was being wheeled out of the operating room.

When Pharmaceuticals Are Not Enough: Electrical and Magnetic Medicine

Despite all we know about neurotransmitters, antidepressants, and genetics, the outcome of antidepressant pharmaceutical treatment is often disappointing. It has been said that one-third of people who take antidepressants get a good effect, one-third get a partial response, and one-third get no noticeable effect.[141] For those who have a poor outcome, sometimes strengthening Layers One and Two of their healing plan can help. For those with debilitating depression who derive no benefit from pharmaceuticals, electrical and magnetic medicine are sometimes considered.

Transcranial Magnetic Stimulation (TMS)

As of this writing, transcranial magnetic stimulation (TMS) is a relative newcomer in the field of electrical and magnetic medicine (also known as *neuromodulation*). The FDA approved TMS for treatment of major depressive disorder in 2008. Before that, it had extensive development and testing in Canada. TMS is specifically indicated for adults who have failed to achieve satisfactory improvement from an antidepressant.[142] TMS is also called rTMS (repetitive transcranial magnetic stimulation).

TMS stimulates small areas of the brain with brief, focused electromagnetic pulses. The strength of the magnetic pulse is about the same as an MRI scan. It's called "repetitive" because the magnetic energy is applied in short bursts over the course of about forty minutes.[143] No anesthesia or muscle relaxant is needed because the magnetic pulse stimulates the electrical connections between nerve cells without inducing a seizure.

For some people, the biggest problems with TMS treatment are time and expense. It is necessary to have treatments five days per week (Monday through Friday) for four to six weeks, and treatment is not always (or completely) covered by health insurance. For those who do not benefit from antidepressants but whose depression is not severe enough to warrant electroconvulsive therapy (ECT), TMS can be a desirable option.

Electroconvulsive Therapy (ECT)

Electroconvulsive therapy (ECT) has been in use since 1938, long before the pharmaceutical antidepressants we have now. A 2012 review of the scientific studies of ECT showed a remission rate of 51 percent for depression,[144] suggesting that it may be superior to pharmaceuticals, particularly for severe depression, which have a remission rate of 40 percent, compared to a remission rate of 25 percent by placebo.[145] Despite ECT's long-term use, the FDA continues to review its safety. Currently classified as a category III device (highest risk category), the FDA is considering reclassifying it in the less restrictive category II for "severe major depressive episode."[146]

Your brain is not just a bag of chemicals. It's also a complex electrical network that can be influenced by external electricity and magnetism. Electricity and magnetism applied externally can both excite the electrons in the membranes of your brain cells.

We know from imaging studies (MRIs and PET scans) that most types of depression involve the left dorsolateral prefrontal cortex (roughly your left temple),[147] along with deeper brain structures, including the amygdala and hippocampus.[148] Delivering an electrical pulse to these areas can result in improvement of depression. It can also cause confusion and memory loss, which usually last only hours or days but can last longer.

ECT has been the subject of considerable scrutiny and criticism by those concerned about its dangers and misuses.[149] ECT has also been credited with helping many who would not have recovered without it.[150]

With ECT, I have seen some people suffer severe memory loss for a prolonged period with little effect on their depression. I have also seen people derive tremendous benefit from ECT with little or no side effects. My recommendation is this: For severe, disabling, and life-threatening depression when pharmaceuticals have not helped, consider ECT. I have seen it save lives and restore the flow of healing when all else has failed.

Psychiatric Medicine's Risks

The decision to take psychiatric medicine should not be made lightly. Medicine can save a life, but it can also take a life. Being well informed about the danger of taking medicine will help you decide whether it's worth the risk.

Considerable literature is available about the risk of taking psychiatric medicine.[151] In addition to many antipsychiatry websites, Dr. Peter Breggin's landmark book *Toxic Psychiatry* points to the dangers of psychiatric medications and makes a strong case against using them.[152] There's even a museum in Los Angeles, California, called Psychiatry: An Industry of Death dedicated to highlighting the dangers and risks of taking psychiatric medicine. It is owned and operated by the Citizens' Commission on Human Rights, founded by the Church of Scientology and psychiatrist Thomas Szasz, who wrote *The Myth of Mental Illness*.[153]

I recommend you do everything you can to enhance and guide your natural flow of healing with the hope of resolving your depression without the use of medicine. If, however, your depression is so severe that it endangers your life or interferes with your lifestyle, medicine may be helpful and necessary. If, despite considerable effort, you cannot seem to talk your way out of being depressed, you may need medicine.

Can Hard Anxiety and Depression Be Softened?

Just as soft anxiety and depression can become hardened by persistent adversity and trauma, hard anxiety and depression can often be softened by persistent healthy behaviors and therapeutic guidance.

As you promote your healing with healthy behaviors and therapeutic guidance, be careful not to prematurely lower the dose or stop taking a medicine that may have been helping you. Stopping medicine too soon can cause a relapse of symptoms.

Hard anxiety or depression typically fluctuates in intensity no matter its cause. Just because a hardened condition seems to dissipate doesn't necessarily mean it's gone for good. The reduced intensity may be due to less stress in your life, successful healing, or a natural rhythm. If your anxiety or depression returns, a medicine that helped before might need to be restarted or the dose of a medicine you're currently taking might need to be increased. I advise you to discuss any medication changes you may be considering with your prescriber as well as with any other professionals involved in your care.

Hard anxiety and depression conditions, especially those genetically inherited, do not easily resolve. By doing everything you can to help yourself heal, you will improve your life, but you may not completely eradicate a genetic condition. Until we are able to change your genetic makeup or better able to influence your genetic expression, medicine may still be needed to manage your symptoms if they are due to hard anxiety or depression.

Genetically Modified Emotions?

We have genetically modified corn, soybeans, and mushrooms; why not genetically modified emotions? Using a technology called CRISPR, scientists have successfully removed a gene that causes a fatal heart defect from human embryos.[154] The embryos were not allowed to develop, but the experiment showed that human gene editing can be done.

The future of medicine requires examination of this question: If we know a gene causes suffering, should it be removed? If you knew your unborn child had a gene that would cause early death, would you want it removed? What if it were a gene that greatly increased your child's risk of suicide or a gene that would likely result in a difficult-to-treat depression?

When the science and technology of human gene editing becomes sophisticated enough to consider genetically modifying human emotions, some difficult ethical questions will need answers as well: Does it represent artificial mind control? Does it assist healing or violate a natural law? Will it become a political tool? These and other questions need not be answered today, but they may need to be addressed eventually.

Meanwhile, the study of gene expression has shown that, to a degree, you can affect whether unwanted genes are switched on and, if they are, what you can do to try to switch them off. Clearly, too much adversity can increase the activity of genes linked to depression. Keeping those genes quiet or dialing down how much they are expressed is part of the benefit of the ABCs of Layer One: Enhancement. If you can maintain healthy attitudes and behaviors and surround yourself with compassionate love, you will reduce the likelihood that unhealthy stress will switch on or dial up your unhealthy genes.

Can Growing Old Heal Your Mind?

There's good news in aging: As you grow older, you are likely to experience greater contentment.[155] Thankfully, as we age, our resilience and capacity to cope with adversity and change strengthen. This may be the best part of growing old. Although you may not do so well physically, odds are your positive feelings about yourself and your life are more likely to increase.

Some say growing old is not for sissies. The good news is that the older you get, the less of a sissy you'll be. Growing old can, at times, be sad and scary. Friends and loved ones die, illnesses develop, and death looms. How, then, can we explain the fact that, for many, aging brings greater contentment?

I've seen it happen many times. As my patients have aged, they often find they don't need as much medicine. Sometimes they stop it altogether. This includes people who previously had severe anxiety or depression. Others, though they may need to continue taking medicine, become more self-confident and accepting.

We don't know if greater contentment with aging is due to higher concentrations of the right chemicals in the brain or to the accumulation of wisdom and resilience. Whatever the cause, you can take comfort in knowing that you are likely to view your life more favorably as you age.

My view is that this very desirable aspect of aging can be enhanced by healing. When you take the proper steps to empower your healing, you live longer and better with more contentment and fulfillment.

Three Layers Assembled: Lisa's Healing Plan

Now that we have worked our way through all three layers of healing, let's take a look at Lisa's healing plan.

It's a healing plan because it works with her natural process of healing. It does not impose; it assists. There's no forcing with a healing plan. Its function is to enhance, guide, and when necessary, restore the natural flow of healing. Adopting this attitude and this intention will help to make it so.

All decisions about helping someone who is suffering should be based upon these questions: What can be done to assist the

*natural flow of healing without blocking, impeding, or derailing
it? In what ways can we help a mind heal itself without harming
it in the process?*

*Lisa's healing plan represents an attempt to do no (or minimal)
harm while assisting healing in every way possible and practical.
Fortunately, Lisa understood the greater benefit of a healing plan
over a treatment plan. She was willing to go for long-term gain over
short-term relief. She had the capacity to be aware of her addictive
urges and to hold them in abeyance. This way she could fuel her
healing and growth with manageable discomfort rather than block
it with the quick fix of drugged relief. As a result, she could devote
her energy of distress to activities that assisted her healing.*

*In Layer One, she followed the ABCs of enhancement. She
maintained proper attitude with self-acceptance, perseverance,
and gratitude. She adopted the healing-enhancing behaviors of
mindfulness, exercise, diet, and stress management (MEDS). She
allowed herself to feel compassionate love from her dog, Ginger, her
friend Rachel, and her rediscovered soul mate, Jake.*

*In Layer Two: Guidance, she pursued a variety of psychotherapies
as her needs shifted. She had as a baseline supportive insight-oriented
therapy. To this, she added, as needed, cognitive behavioral therapy,
group therapy, codependency workshops, and self-help meetings. She
developed her spiritual practice by intensifying her work with a yoga
therapist and by attending spiritual retreats.*

*She added Layer Three: Restoration only when necessary for
her genetic depression. When symptoms of her depression blocked
her capacity to effectively engage in Layer One: Enhancement and
Layer Two: Guidance, medication helped her get back on track.
Carefully chosen medication reduced her symptoms enough to*

restore her flow of healing. Then she could make sense of what was being processed in therapy and she could engage more actively in the healing-enhancing activities of exercise and meditation.

Fortunately, Lisa was able to benefit enough from Layers One and Two to heal and restructure her life so that she could reduce and then stop medicine between recurrences of depression. She was also able to stop medicine when she and Jake decided to start a family. Although her obstetrician had agreed to work with a carefully chosen antidepressant if needed, she managed to make use of Layer One plus Layer Two well enough not to need medicine.

The field of mind healing is full of fascination and uncertainty. Despite advances in neuroscience, we still have much to learn. Clearly your mind is capable of healing itself with your help. Usually this can be done without medicine. When medicine is needed, it can usually reduce symptoms enough to restore your flow of healing. Then you can take on life's daily challenges. Restoration of healing with medicine, when needed, can be a sensible and effective component of a successful healing plan.

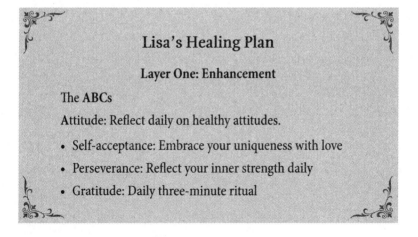

Lisa's Healing Plan

Layer One: Enhancement

The ABCs

Attitude: Reflect daily on healthy attitudes.

- Self-acceptance: Embrace your uniqueness with love
- Perseverance: Reflect your inner strength daily
- Gratitude: Daily three-minute ritual

Behavior: MEDS
- Mindfulness: Meditate at least three minutes daily; attend to the moment
- Exercise: Three minutes of exertion daily plus other workouts
- Diet: No sugar, low gluten, low-inflammatory diet
- Stress Management: Stay below stress threshold

Compassionate love
- Practice self-forgiveness
- Spend time with people who love you
- Fall in love

Layer Two: Guidance

Cognitive
- Psychotherapy: Continue individual psychotherapy and codependency group therapy
- Use cognitive behavioral therapy (CBT) as needed for ruminations

Body and Energy Work
- Therapeutic massage as needed or desired
- Acupressure for quick relief of anxiety

Spiritual
- Develop yoga practice and meditation
- Spend time with nature

Layer Three: Restoration

Medicine: Antidepressants for genetic depression
- Reduce dose if it interferes with Layers One and Two because of emotional blunting as long as depression does not worsen

Afterword

Three Layers of Healing for Your Body

Now that you've learned how to construct a Three-Layered Healing Plan for anxiety and depression, you can use the same method to create a Three-Layered Healing Plan for any physical illness or injury you might experience. Layer by layer you can add wellness activities, therapy treatments, and medicines as needed and as relevant for your medical ailments. Using the basic principles of enhancement, guidance, and restoration of healing, you can organize and strengthen your approach and your treatment team's approach to any medical condition you may have.

Layer One

Your body did not come equipped with a manual for proper care and use, but you can create your own with the healing enhancements of Layer One. The ABCs of healing enhancement—positive attitudes, healthy behaviors, and compassionate love—promote healing of physical as well as psychological distress. Diabetes specialists tell their patients to exercise and eat well to help manage their blood sugar. Rheumatologists tell their patients to do the same to reduce inflammation. Cardiologists recommend Layer One's healing enhancements to help their patients manage their hypertension and heart conditions. Primary care providers recommend healing enhancements for their patients' overall health. Practicing Layer One's healing enhancements creates a strong base of healing for any medical condition.

If you incorporate healing enhancements in your daily routine, you may be able to prevent medical problems from developing in the first place. Eating well, exercising regularly, and lowering stress may reduce your likelihood of developing diabetes, high blood pressure, or stress-related gastrointestinal problems. If, despite following a Layer One wellness plan, you develop a chronic medical problem like hypertension, diabetes, irritable bowel syndrome (IBS), or gastroesophageal reflux disease (GERD), you can reduce the severity of your condition and hasten your recovery by taking better care of yourself.

Layer Two

If it's hard for you to adhere to your Layer One wellness plan, or if you're not sure what type of meditation, exercise, or diet is right for you and your medical condition, I recommend you reach out to a Layer Two practitioner for guidance. Depending upon the type of condition or ailment you need to treat or manage, a relevant Layer Two practitioner might be a nutritionist, a physical therapist, a physical trainer, or a dental hygienist.

A nutritionist can help you design a diet that will help prevent or manage diabetes, hypertension, IBS, or GERD. A physical therapist might help you avoid back or joint surgery or might help you recover from it. If you have an autoimmune disorder, helpful Layer Two practitioners—including nurses, nutritionists, physical trainers, and yoga therapists—can help you construct your Layer One meditation, exercise, diet, and stress management program to lower your inflammation. If you have heart disease or cancer, nutritionists and exercise trainers can help you design safe diets and exercises to complement and empower the effectiveness of any medical treatments you may be receiving.

Layer Two practitioners can also help guide you as you decide what medical treatment may be best. Many medical and surgical practices have access to nurses, nutritionists, and other licensed or certified Layer Two practitioners who can help you focus your treatment plan and your healing plan to optimize your recovery. Layer Two practitioners can encourage you to continue your healthy lifestyle changes. I encourage you to share your healing plan with your treatment providers and ask them for suggestions. I especially recommend that you show your doctors your Three-Layered Healing Plan. They might have something to add, and it's important that they know what diet, exercise, and other healing methods you may be using.

When my dental hygienist asked me about *Mind Easing*, I told her it's about a Three-Layered Healing Plan for anxiety and depression. I also told her that the concept of a Three-Layered Healing Plan is not limited to mental health and that I am also using a Three-Layered Healing Plan for my dental health. I told my dental hygienist that she is my Layer Two healing guide for my teeth and gums. She uses noninvasive therapies to thoroughly clean my teeth and help rejuvenate my gums. She also reminds me each time I see her what I can do to improve my dental health with healthy eating and regular brushing, flossing, and gargling (my Layer One dental healing enhancements). Because of my efforts to enhance my dental health and thanks to her guidance, I spend less time in my dentist's surgery chair for drillings and crowns. Seeing my dentist for invasive procedures like fillings and crowns represents Layer Three: Restoration as applied to dentistry.

Layer Three

With physical illness and injuries, Layer Three: Restoration includes pharmaceuticals and surgeries. As with anxiety and depression, Layer Three treatments should be reserved for problems that do not respond to Layers One and Two alone. Examples of Layer Three interventions include antibiotics for unresolved bacterial infections; blood sugar–lowering medicines for diabetes; medicine for persistently elevated blood pressure; surgery, radiation and/or chemotherapy for cancer; and medicine and surgery for blocked coronary arteries or malfunctioning heart valves.

Having a healing plan can be comforting if you have a life-threatening illness. Your healing plan can help you feel empowered and focused on getting well when you might otherwise feel weak and scared. You place yourself in a position of greater empowerment when you actively suggest Layer One wellness and Layer Two therapeutic activities that complement the treatment decisions that you and your doctor make.

No matter how many of the three layers of healing you may need for your body or your mind, you should revise your Three-Layered Healing Plan as often as needed. The specific components of your Three-Layered Healing Plan will likely change over time. Your healing plan will be influenced by your health, events in your life, and advances in medical treatment. For example, as discoveries are made in epigenetics (how genetic expression can be modified by your lifestyle), you will find out more about which types of food, exercise, and meditation are best for your genetic profile. As techniques in psychotherapy, physical therapy, and other forms of Layer Two guidance are refined, you may find new approaches that will more effectively help resolve your physical and emotional distress, hopefully with less need for medicine or surgery. As the field of medicine becomes more personalized with treatments targeted to your genotype, medicines will become safer and more effective. By harmonizing your medical treatment with your healing enhancements and healing guides, you'll complement your natural flow of healing and optimize your recovery.

The Three-Layered Healing Plan
for Medical Conditions

Layer One: Enhancement

Attitudes (chapter 4): Self-acceptance, perseverance, and gratitude will help you heal your body as well as your mind.

Behaviors (chapter 5): Mindfulness, Exercise, Diet, and Stress management (MEDS) will empower your healing. Discuss exercise and diet specifics with your treatment providers.

Compassionate love (chapter 6): Spend time with people and creatures who love you and care about you.

Layer Two: Guidance

Continue whatever forms of guidance are helping you reduce anxiety and depression. Depending upon your medical condition, schedule time with professionals who do not prescribe medicine to address nonmedicinal aspects of your treatment. These may include nutritionists, physical therapists, genetic counselors, acupuncturists, chiropractors, and yoga therapists.

Layer Three: Restoration

Pharmaceutical or surgical approaches may be necessary depending upon the nature of your condition if Layers One and Two are insufficient for reducing your symptoms or reversing the cause of your condition. Be sure to discuss your healing plan with your Layer Three treatment providers. They may have suggestions for you about fine-tuning Layer One and Layer Two in order to complement what pharmaceutical or surgical interventions you may need.

Acknowledgments

I *am honored and humbled by* the courageous men and women who have come to me for help with healing. Their honesty and vulnerability have touched me and inspired me, and it is because of them that I feel emboldened to do as much as I can to help relieve suffering for as many as I can by writing this book.

I am grateful to the many writers and teachers who have influenced me over the years. They have helped me develop a critical (and at times skeptical) eye as I evaluate those methods of assisting healing that show evidence of effectiveness. I credit those writers and teachers for giving me the information and training I've needed to develop and mature my own ideas about how to assist healing.

I am forever grateful to the many skillful and caring practitioners and friends who have helped me with my own healing. It is because of their capabilities and compassion that I have become better equipped to manage life's challenges and to find my way to greater ease. They have expanded my awareness of the many ways healing can be assisted, and they have shown me how important it is to persevere despite adversity.

I give thanks to my wife, Ramona (aka Romcha), for her loving support and encouragement and for patiently and honestly responding to my persistent question, "How does this sound?" Her insights about human nature and her artistic eye and ear for style have been immensely helpful.

I thank my daughters, who cheered me on as I wrote *Mind Easing*. They are bright and beautiful women who grace the world with their love, strength, and kindness.

I thank my parents, Walter Wanck and Beatrice Dewey Wanck. They never stopped loving and supporting me despite their struggles and the challenges I gave them. They showed me that with persistence, faith, and love, adversity can be managed if not overcome.

My developmental editor and writing coach, Candace Johnson at Change It Up Editing, helped me find my voice and my love of writing. She patiently and kindly guided me as I stumbled through years of writing and rewriting. Her skill as a guide has been immensely valuable, as has her warmth as a good friend. *Mind Easing* would not exist if it weren't for Candace. I will always be grateful to my friend and colleague Patricia O'Gorman, PhD, author of *The Resilient Woman*, for introducing us.

I thank my editor, Allison Janse, at Health Communications Incorporated (HCI) for sharing my vision that *Mind Easing* could help heal suffering. Allison and the talented staff of HCI have transformed *Mind Easing* into a visually appealing and easily accessible book. I am honored to join the HCI community.

I'm grateful to my assistant, Amanda Hall, for laboriously transcribing my scribbled longhand, for her very helpful comments about *Mind Easing,* and for her undying enthusiasm for the project.

I thank my staff and colleagues, who over the years have patiently and enthusiastically supported me and shared their knowledge and skills. Their insights and suggestions about assisting healing have been enormously helpful, and I am honored to work with them.

Many thanks to the guys in the "men's group." For thirty years we six leaderless friends have been meeting monthly to support and encourage one another. Together we suffer tragedies and celebrate victories as brothers.

Profound thanks to my many friends and relatives who have graced my life with love.

Above all, I give thanks to the invisible force that creates life and channels healing.

Bick Wanck, MD
Saratoga Springs, NY, Autumnal Equinox 2018

Notes

1   Wray N, et al. "Genetic relationship between five psychiatric disorders estimated from genome-wide SNPs." *Nature Genetics* 45 (August 2013): 984–94.

2   Kübler-Ross E. *On Death and Dying*. New York: MacMillan Publishing Co., 1969.

3   Harvard Medical School, 2007. National Comorbidity Survey (NCS). (2017, August 21). Retrieved from https://www.hcp.med.harvard.edu/ncs/index.php. Data Table 1: Lifetime prevalence DSM-IV /WMH-CIDI disorders by sex and cohort. Retrieved from nimh.nih.gov.

4   Emmons RA, McCullough ME, eds. New York: *The Psychology of Gratitude*. Oxford University Press, 2004.

5   Amin A. *The Science of Gratitude: More Benefits Than Expected; 26 Studies and Counting*. http://happier human.com/the-science-of-gratitude/.

6   McCullough M, Emmons R, Tsang J. "The grateful disposition: A conceptual and empirical topography." *Journal of Personality and Social Psychology* 82, no. 1 (2002): 112–27. doi: 10.1037//0022 -3514.82.1.112.

7   McCullough M, Emmons R. "Counting blessings versus burdens: An experimental investigation of gratitude and subjective well-being in daily life." *Journal of Personality and Social Psychology* 84, no. 2 (2003): 377–89. doi: 10.1037/0022-3514.84.2.377.

8   Hoge EA, et al. "Randomized control trial of mindfulness meditation for generalized anxiety disorder: Effects on anxiety and stress reactivity." *Journal of Clinical Psychiatry* 74, no. 8 (August 2013): 786–92.

9   Kalima P, et al. "Rapid changes in histone deacetylases and inflammatory gene expression in expert meditators." *Psychoneuroendocrinology* 40 (February 2014): 96–107.

10 Black D, et al. "Yogic meditation reverses NF-KB and IRF-related transcriptome dynamics in leukocytes of family dementia caregivers in a randomized controlled trial." *Psychoneuroendocrinology* 38, no. 3 (March 2013): 348–55.

11 Pica T. "Stalking the meditating brain." *Mindful*, August 2014, 51–57.

12 Erikson K, et al. "Exercise training increases size of hippocampus and improves memory." *Proceedings of the National Academy of Science U.S.A.* 108, no. 7 (February 2011): 3017–22.

13 Cotman C, Berchtold N. "Exercise: A behavioral intervention to enhance brain health and plasticity." *Trends in Neurosciences* 25, no. 6 (June 2002): 295–301.

[14] Tabata I, et al. "Effects of moderate-intensity endurance and high-intensity intermittent training on anaerobic capacity and VO2max." *Medicine & Science in Sports & Exercise* 28, no. 10 (October 1996): 1327–30.

[15] Emberts T, et al. "Exercise intensity and energy expenditure of a Tabata workout." *Journal of Sports Science & Medicine* 12, no. 3 (September 2013): 612–13.

[16] Trivedi MH, et al. "Exercise as an augmentation treatment for nonremitted major depressive disorder: A randomized, parallel-dose comparison." *Journal of Clinical Psychiatry* 72, no. 5 (May 2011): 677–84.

[17] Harvey SB, et al. "Exercise and the prevention of depression: Results of the HUNT cohort study." *American Journal of Psychiatry* 175, no. 1 (January 1, 2018): 28–36. doi: 10.1176/appi.ajp.2017.16111223. Epub October 3, 2017.

[18] Carek PJ, Laibstain SE, Carek SM. "Exercise for the treatment of depression and anxiety." *International Journal of Psychiatry in Medicine* 41, no. 1 (2011): 15–28.

[19] Broocks A, et al. "Comparison of aerobic exercise, clomipramine, and placebo in the treatment of panic disorder." *American Journal of Psychiatry* 155, no. 5 (1998): 603–9.

[20] Jackson JR, et al. "Neurologic and psychiatric manifestations of celiac disease and gluten sensitivity." *Psychiatric Quarterly* 83, no. 1. (March 2012): 91–102. doi: 10.1007/s11126-011-9186-y.

[21] Perlmutter D. *Grain Brain.* New York: Little, Brown, and Company, 2013.

[22] DeBerardis D, et al. "The effect of newer serotonin-noradrenalin antidepressants on cytokine production: A review of the current literature." *International Journal of Immunopathology and Pharmacology* 23, no. 2 (April–June 2010): 417–22. doi: 10.1177/039463201002300204.

[23] Martinez-Gonzalez MA, et. al. "Benefits of the Mediterranean diet: Insights from the PREDIMED study." *Progress in Cardiovascular Diseases* 58, no. 1 (July–August 2015): 58(1): 50–60. doi: 10.1016/j.pcad.2015.04.003.

[24] Estruch R, et al. "Primary prevention of cardiovascular disease with a Mediterranean diet." *New England Journal of Medicine* 368 (April 4, 2013): 1279–90. doi: 10.1056/NEJMoa1200303.

[25] Sanchez-Villegas A, et al. "Mediterranean dietary pattern and depression: The PREDIMED randomized trial." *BMC Medicine* 11, no. 208 (September 20, 2013). doi: 10.1186/1741-7015-11-208.

[26] Stoll AL, et al. "Omega 3 fatty acids in bipolar disorder: A preliminary double-blind, placebo-controlled trial." *Archives of General Psychiatry* 56, no. 5 (May 1999): 407–12.

[27] Jazayeri S. "Comparison of therapeutic effects of omega-3 fatty acid eicosapentaenoic acid and fluoxetine, separately and in combination, in major depressive disorder." *Australian and New Zealand Journal of Psychiatry* 42, no. 3 (March 2008): 192–98.

[28] Li Y. "Fish consumption and severely depressed mood: Findings from the first national nutrition follow-up study." *Psychiatry Research* 190, no. 1 (November 2011): 103–9.

[29] Parker G, et al. "Omega-3 fatty acids and mood disorders." *American Journal of Psychiatry* 163, no. 6 (June 2006): 969–78.

[30] Hibbeln J. "Fish consumption and major depression." *The Lancet* 351, no. 9110 (April 18, 1998): 1213.

[31] Michalak J, Zhang XC, Jacobi F. "Vegetarian diet and mental disorders: Results from a representative community survey." *International Journal of Behavioral Nutrition and Physical Activity* 9 (2012): 67. doi:10.1186/1479-5868-9-67.

[32] Beezhold B, et al. "Vegetarian diets are associated with healthy mood states: A cross-sectional study in Seventh Day Adventist adults." *Nutrition Journal* 9 (2010): 26.

[33] Norris J. "Omega-3 fatty acid recommendations for vegetarians." VeganHealth.org. April 2014.

[34] Seader R, Fuchs S, Milo R. Revised estimates for the number of human and bacterial cells in the body. *Public Library of Science-Biology* 14, no. 8 (August 2016): e1002533. doi: 10.1371/journal.pbio.1002533.

[35] Selhub E, Logan A, Bested A. Fermented foods, microbiota, and mental health: Ancient practice meets nutritional psychiatry." *Journal of Physiological Anthropology* 33, no. 2 (2014). http://www.physiobanthropol.com/content/33/1/2.

[36] Dinan TG, et al. "Collective unconscious: How gut microbes shape human behavior." *Journal of Psychiatric Research* 63 (April 2015): 1–9. doi: 10.1016/j.jpsychires.2015.02.021. Epub March 3, 2015.

[37] Pinto-Sanchez MI, Hall GB, et al. "Probiotic *Bifidobacterium longum* NCC3001 reduces depression scores and alters brain activity: A pilot study in patients with irritable bowel syndrome." *Gastroenterology* 153, no. 2 (August 2017): 448–59.e8. doi: 10.1053/jgastro.2017.05.003. Epub May 5, 2017.

[38] https://www.sleepassociation.org/how-many-hours-of-sleep-do-i-need/.

[39] Krznaric, R. *How Should We Live? Great Ideas from the Past for Everyday Life.* BlueBridge, 2013.

[40] Fehr B, Sprecher S, Underwood LG, eds. *The science of compassionate love: Theory, research, and applications.* Malden, MA: Wiley-Blackwell, 2008.

[41] Post, SG, et al. *Altruism and Altruistic Love: Science, Philosophy, and Religion in Dialogue.* Oxford University Press, USA, 2002.

[42] Pace TWW, et al. "Effect of compassion meditation on neuroendocrine, innate immune, and behavioral responses to psychosocial stress." *Psychoendocrinology* 34, no. 1 (January 2009): 83–98. doi:10.1016/j.psyneuen.2008.08.011. Epub October 4, 2008.

[43] Walsh F. "Animal companionship." *Family Process* 48 (2009): 462–80, 481–99.

[44] Beetz A, et al. "Psychosocial and psychophysiological effects of human-animal interactions: the possible role of oxytocin." *Frontiers in Psychology* 3 (2012): 234. http://doi.org/10.3389/fpsyg.2012.00234.

[45] Wisdom JP, et al. "Another breed of 'service' animals: STARS study findings about pet ownership and recovery from serious mental illness." *American Journal of Orthopsychiatry* 79, no. 3 (July 2009): 430–36.

[46] Yong MH, Ruffman T. "Emotional contagion: dogs and humans show a similar physiologic response to human infant crying." *Behavioral Processes* 108 (October 2014): 155–65. doi: 10.1016/j.beproc.2014.10.006. Epub November 4, 2014.

[47] Rosenzweig, MR. "Aspects of the search for neural mechanisms of memory." *Annual Review of Psychology* 47 (1996): 1–32.

[48] Konorski, J. *Conditioned reflexes and neuron organization.* New York: Cambridge University Press, 1948.

[49] Draganski B, et al. "Temporal and spatial dynamics of brain structure changes during extensive learning." *Journal of Neuroscience* 26, no. 23 (June 2006): 6314–17.

[50] Linden DE. "How psychotherapy changes the brain: The contribution of functional neuroimaging." *Molecular Psychiatry* 11, no. 6 (2006): 528–38.

[51] Karlsson H. "How psychotherapy changes the brain." *Psychiatric Times.* August 11, 2011.

[52] DeRubeis R, Hollon S, Ansterdand JD, et al. "Cognitive therapy vs. medications in the treatment of moderate to severe depression." *Archives of General Psychiatry* 62, no. 4 (2005): 409–16.

[53] Hollon SD, et al. "Prevention of relapse following cognitive therapy vs. medications in moderate to severe depression." *Archives of General Psychiatry* 62, no. 4 (2005): 417–22.

[54] Mayo-Wilson, E, Dias S, Mavranezoluli I, et al. "Psychological and pharmacological interventions for social anxiety disorder in adults: A systematic review and network meta-analysis." *The Lancet Psychiatry* 1, no. 5 (2014): 368–76.

[55] Shalev A, et al. "Prevention of posttraumatic stress disorder by early treatment." *Archives of General Psychiatry* 69, no. 2 (2011): 166–76.

[56] Simpson HB, Foa E, Liebowitz MR, et al. "Cognitive-behavioral therapy vs. risperidone for augmenting serotonin preuptake inhibitors in obsessive-compulsive disorder. A randomized clinical trial." *JAMA Psychiatry* 70, no. 11 (2013): 1190–98.

[57] Keller M, McCullough J, Klein D, et al. "A comparison of nefazodone, the cognitive behavioral-analysis system of psychotherapy, and their combination for the treatment of chronic depression." *New England Journal of Medicine* 342 (May 18, 2000): 1462–70.

[58] Steinert C, et al. "Psychodynamic therapy: As efficacious as other empirically supported treatments? A meta-analysis testing equivalence of outcomes." *American Journal of Psychiatry* 174 (2017): 943–53. doi: 10.0076/appi.ajp.2017.17010057.

[59] Gloster AT, Sonntag R, Hoyer J, et al. "Treating treatment-resistant patients with panic disorder and agoraphobia using psychotherapy: A randomized controlled switching trial." *Psychotherapy and Psychosomatics* 84 (2015): 100–109.

[60] Shapiro F. *Eye movement desensitization and reprocessing: Basic principles, protocols and procedures*, 2nd ed. New York: Guilford Press, 2001.

[61] Shapiro F. "Efficacy of the eye movement desensitization procedure in the treatment of traumatic memories." *Journal of Trauma Stress* 2, no. 2 (1989): 199–223.

[62] Foa EB, Keane TM, Friedman MJ. *Effective Treatments for PTSD: Practice Guidelines of the International Society for Traumatic Stress Studies*. New York: Guilford Press, 2009.

[63] Van der Kolk BA, Spinazzola J, et al. "A randomized clinical trial of eye movement desensitization and reprocessing (EMDR), fluoxetine, and pill placebo in the treatment of posttraumatic stress disorder: Treatment effects and long term maintenance." *Journal of Clinical Psychiatry* 68, no. 1 (2007): 37–46.

[64] Wanck B. "Mentally ill chemical abusers." In *Handbook of Outpatient Treatment of Adults*. M Thase, B Edelstein, M Hersen, eds. New York: Plenum Press, 1990.

[65] Ma K-W. "The roots and development of Chinese acupuncture from prehistory to the early 20th century." *Acupuncture in Medicine* 10 (1992): 92–99.

[66] Prioreschi P. *A History of Medicine*, vol. 2. Omaha: Horatius Press, 2004, 147–48.

[67] Moyer CA, et al. "A meta-analysis of massage therapy research." *Psychological Bulletin* 130, no. 1 (2004): 3–18.

[68] Colquhound, N. "Acupuncture is a theatrical placebo: The end of a myth." *Analgesia and Anesthesia* 116, no. 6 (2013): 1360–63.

[69] Ernst E, Lee MS, Chai T-Y. (2010). "Acupuncture for depression? A systematic review of systematic reviews." *Evaluation and the Health Professions* 34, no. 4 (2011): 403–12.

[70] Zhang Z, Chen H-Y, Yip K-C, et al. "The effectiveness and safety of acupuncture therapy in depressive disorders: Systematic review and meta-analysis." *Journal of Affective Disorders* 124, no. 1–2 (July 2010): 9–21.

[71] Wang H, et al. "Is acupuncture beneficial in depression: A meta-analysis of eight randomized controlled trials." *Journal of Affective Disorders* (2008), doi: https://doi.org/10.1016/j.jad.2008.04.020

[72] Chan YY, et al. "The benefit of combined acupuncture and antidepressant medication for depression: a systematic review and meta-analysis." *Journal of Affective Disorders* (May 2015): 106–117. doi 10–1016/j.jad.2015.01.048.

[73] Errington-Evans N. "Acupuncture for anxiety." *CNS Neuroscience and Therapeutics* 18, no. 4 (2011): 277–84.

[74] Hollifield M, et al. (2007). "Acupuncture for posttraumatic stress disorder: A randomized controlled pilot trial." *Journal of Mental and Nervous Disorders* 195, no. 6 (June 2007): 504–13.

[75] Hui KK, Lin J, et al. "Acupuncture modulates the limbic system and subcortical gray structure of the human brain: Evidence from fMRI studies in normal subjects." *Human Brain Mapping* 9, no. 1 (2000): 13–25.

[76] Dhond RP, et al. "Neuroimaging acupuncture effects in the human brain." *Journal of Alternative and Complementary Medicine* 13, no. 6 (2007): 603–16.

[77] http://www.modernreflexology.com/acupressure-to-relieve-anxiety-palpitations-and-nervousness/.

[78] Shapiro D, Cook I, Abrams M. "Yoga as complementary treatment of depression: Effects of traits and moods on treatment outcome." *Evidence-Based Complementary and Alternative Medicine* 4, no. 4 (2007): 493–502.

[79] Khuar SS, Kaur P, Kaur S. "Effectiveness of Shavasana on depression among university students." *Indian Journal of Clinical Psychology* 20 (1993): 82–87.

[80] Janakiramaiah N, et al. "Antidepressant efficacy of Sudarshan Kriya yoga (SKY) in melancholia: A randomized comparison with electroconvulsive therapy (ECT) and imipramine." *Journal of Affective Disorders* 57 (2000): 255–59.

[81] Dossey L. *Prayer Is Good Medicine.* New York: Harper Collins, 1996.

[82] Astin JE, et al. "The efficacy of 'distant healing': A systematic review of randomized trials." *Annals of Internal Medicine* 142 (2000): 903.

[83] Church D. *The Genie in Your Genes: Epigenetic Medicine and the New Biology of Intention.* Energy Psychology Press, 2008.

[84] Ellison C, Bradshaw M, Flannelly K, Galek K. "Prayer, attachment to God, and symptoms of anxiety-related disorders among U.S. adults." *Sociology of Religion* 75, no. 2 (2014): 208–33. doi: 10.1093/socrel/srt079.

[85] Miller L, et al. "Religiosity and major depression in adults at high risk: A ten-year prospective study." *American Journal of Psychiatry* 169, no. 1 (2012): 89–94.

[86] Miller L, et al. "Neuroanatomical correlates of religiosity and spirituality: A study in adults at high and low familial risk for depression." *JAMA Psychiatry* 71, no. 2 (2014): 128–35.

[87] Harner M. *The Way of the Shaman.* 3rd ed. HarperSanFrancisco, 1990.

[88] Scott, GG. *The Complete Idiot's Guide to Shamanism.* Alpha Publishing, 2002.

[89] Nortje G, et al. "Effectiveness of traditional healers in treating mental disorders: A systematic review." *The Lancet Psychiatry* 3 (2016): 154–70.

[90] Ingerman S. *Shamanic Journeying: A Beginner's Guide.* Sounds True, 2008.

[91] Park BJ, et al. "The physiological effects of *shinrin-yoku* (taking in the forest atmosphere or forest bathing): Evidence from field experiments in 24 forests across Japan." *Environmental Health and Preventive Medicine* 15, no. 1 (January 2010): 18–26. doi: 10.1007/512199-009-0086-9.

[92] Hollon SD, et al. "Effect of cognitive therapy with antidepressant medications vs. antidepressants alone on the rate of recovery in major depressive disorder: A randomized controlled trial." *JAMA Psychiatry* 71, no. 10 (October 2014): 1157–64. doi:10.1001/jamapsychiatry2014.1054.

[93] Parker V, et al. "Adverse reactions to St. John's Wort." *Canadian Journal of Psychiatry* 46, no. 1 (2001): 77–79.

[94] Linde K, Berner M, Egger M, Mulrow C. "St. John's Wort for depression: Meta-analysis of randomized controlled trials." *British Journal of Psychiatry* 186, no. 2 (2005): 99–107.

[95] Ernst E, et al. "Adverse effects profile of the herbal antidepressant St. John's Wort (Hypericum perforation L)." *European Journal of Clinical Pharmacology* 54, no. 8 (1998): 589–94.

[96] Lopresti A, Drummond P. "Saffron (*Crocus sativus*) for depression: A systematic review of clinical studies and examination of underlying antidepressant mechanisms of action." *Human Psychopharmacology: Clinical and Experimental* 29, no. 6 (2014): 517–27.

[97] Ibid.

[98] Ibid.

[99] Ibid.

[100] Kulkarnisk, DA. "An overview of curcumin in neurological disorders." *Indian Journal of Pharmaceutical Sciences* 72, no. 2 (2010): 149–54.

[101] Lopresti A. "Curcumin for the treatment of major depression: A randomized, double-blind, placebo controlled study." *Journal of Affective Disorders* 167 (2014): 368–75.

[102] Sanmukhani J, et al. "Efficacy and safety of curcumin in major depressive disorder: A randomized controlled trial." *Phytotherapy Research* 28, no. 4 (2014): 579–85.

[103] Amsterdam JD, et al. "Randomized, double-blind, placebo-controlled trial of *Matricaria recutita* (chamomile) extract therapy for generalized anxiety disorder." *Journal of Clinical Psychopharmacology* 29 (2009): 378–82.

[104] Volz HP, Kieser M. "Kava-kava extract WS1490 versus placebo in anxiety disorders: A randomized placebo-controlled 25-week outpatient trial." *Pharmacopsychiatry* 30, no. 1 (1997): 1–5.

[105] Singh YN, Singh NN. "Therapeutic potential of kava in the treatment of anxiety disorders." *CNS Drugs* 16, no. 11 (2002): 731–43.

[106] Akhondzadeh S, et al. "Passionflower in the treatment of generalized anxiety: A pilot double-blind randomized controlled trial with oxazepam." *Journal of Clinical Pharmacy and Therapeutics* 26, no. 5 (2001): 369–73.

[107] Weeks BS. "Formulations of dietary supplements and herbal extracts for relaxation and anxiolytic action: Valerian." *Medical Science Monitor* 15, no. 11 (2009): 256–62.

[108] Holzl J, Godau P. "Receptor binding studies with *Valeriana officinalis* on the benzodiazepine receptor." *Planta Medica* 55, no. 7 (1989): 642.

[109] Mennini T, et al. "In vitro study in the interaction of extracts and pure compounds from *Valerian a officinalis* roots with GABA, benzodiazepine, and barbiturate receptors." *Fitoterapia* 64 (1993): 291–300.

[110] Garges HP, et al. "Cardiac complications and delirium associated with valerian root withdrawal." *JAMA* 280 (1998): 1566–67.

[111] Rosenthal N. *Winter Blues: Everything You Needed to Know to Beat Seasonal Affective Disorder.* New York: Guilford Press, 2013.

[112] Boyce P, Parker G. "Seasonal affective disorder in the southern hemisphere." *American Journal of Psychiatry* 145, no. 1 (January 1988): 96–99.

[113] Rosenthal. *Winter Blues.*

[114] "FDA proposes new warnings about suicide thinking, behavior in young adults who take antidepressant medication." *FDA News & Events*, U.S. Food and Drug Administration. May 2, 2007.

[115] Sondergard L, et al. "Do antidepressants prevent suicide?" *International Clinical Psychopharmacology* 21, no. 4 (July 2006): 211–18.

[116] Serani D. "On the couch . . . with Dick Cavett." *Psychology Today.* April 21, 2011.

[117] Weaver IC, et al. "Epigenetic programming by maternal behavior." *Nature Neuroscience* 7, no. 8 (2004): 847–54. Epub June 27, 2004.

[118] Ibid.

[119] McGowan PO, et al. "Epigenetic regulation of the glucocorticoid receptor in human brain associates with childhood abuse." *Nature Neuroscience* 12, no. 3 (2009): 342–48. doi:10.10381nn.2270.

[120] Young EA, Abelson JC, Curtis GC, Nesse RM. "Childhood adversity and vulnerability to mood and anxiety disorders." *Depression and Anxiety* 5, no. 2 (1997): 66–72.

[121] Lin JE, Neylan TC, Epel E, O'Donovan A. "Associations of childhood adversity and adulthood trauma with C-reactive protein: A cross-sectional population-based study. *Brain, Behavior, and Immunity* 53 (March 2016): 105–12. doi:10.1016/j.bbi.2015.11.

[122] Phelps J. "The serotonin transporter gene: What's new?" *Psychiatric Times.* October 2, 2015.

[123] Phelps J. "Knowing one's genome: Are we ready?" *Psychiatric Times.* July 31, 2015.

[124] Caspi A, Sugden K, Moffitt TE, et al. "Influence of life stress on depression: Moderation by a polymorphism in the 5-HTT gene." *Science* 301 (2003): 386–89.

[125] Benedetti F, Riccaboni R, Poletti S, et al. "The serotonin transporter genotype modulates the relationship between early stress and adult suicidality in bipolar disorder." *Bipolar Disorders* 16 (2014): 857–66.

[126] Belsky J, Janassaint C, Pluess M, et al. "Vulnerability genes or plasticity genes?" *Molecular Psychiatry* 14 (2009): 746–54.

[127] Kogan SM, Beach SR, Philbert RA, et al. "5-HTTLPR status moderates the effect of early adolescent substance use on risky sexual behavior." *Health Psychology* 29 (2010): 471–76.

[128] Lowe D. "The end of the serotonin transporter gene story? In the pipeline." April 6, 2017. *Science* blog. http://blogs.sciencemag.org/pipeline/archives/2017/04/06/the-end-of-the-serotonin-transporter-gene-story.

[129] Lohoff FW. "Overview of the genetics of major depressive disorder." *Current Psychiatry Reports* 12, no. 6 (2010): 539–46. doi: 10.1007/sll920-010-0150-6.

[130] Singh AB, et al. "Effects of persisting emotional impact from child abuse and norepinephrine transporter genetic variation on antidepressant efficacy in major depression: A pilot study." *Clinical Psychopharmacology and Neuroscience* 13, no. 1 (April 2015): 53–61.

[131] Marshe VS, Maciukiewicz M, Rej S, et al. "Norepinephrine transporter gene variants and remission from depression with venlafaxine treatment in older adults." *American Journal of Psychiatry* 174, no. 5 (May 2017): 468–75.

[132] Hamilton SP, Fyer AJ, Durner M, et al. "Further genetic evidence for a panic disorder syndrome mapping to chromosome 13q." *Proceedings of the National Academy of Sciences USA* 100 (2003): 2550–55.

[133] www.accessdata.fda.gov>daf.

[134] Guzman F. "Aripiprazole indications: FDA-approved and off-label uses." Psychopharmacology Institute. July 18, 2017.

[135] Schrauzer GN, Shrestha KP. "Lithium in drinking water and the incidences of crimes, suicides, and arrests related to drug addictions." *Biological Trace Element Research* 25, no. 2 (May 1990): 105–13.

[136] Lewitzka U, et al. "The suicide prevention effect of lithium: more than 20 years of evidence—a narrative review." International Journal of Bipolar Disorders, 15, no. 3 (March 2015): doi: 10.1186/s403 45-015-0032-2.

[137] Smoller JW, et al. "Cross-Disorder Group of the Psychiatric Genomics Consortium. Identification of risk loci with shared effects on five major psychiatric disorders: A genome-wide analysis." *The Lancet* 381, no. 9875 (April 20, 2013): 1371–79. doi: http://dx.doi.org/10.1016/S0140-6736(12)62129-1.

[138] Benedetti F, Riccaboni R, Poletti S, et al. "The serotonin transporter genotype modulates the relationship between early stress and adult suicidality in bipolar disorder." *Bipolar Disorders* 16 (2014): 857–66.

[139] Perliso R. "Cytochrome P450 genotyping and antidepressants." *BMJ* 334, no. 7597 (April 14, 2007): 759. doi: 10.1136;bmj.39169.547512.80.

[140] Mayo Clinic. "Cytochrome P450 (CYP450) tests." *Mayo Clinic Health Letter.* August 21, 2015.

[141] Trivedi MH, Rush AJ, et al. "Evaluation of outcomes with citalopram for depression using measurement-based care in STAR*D: Implications for clinical practice." *American Journal of Psychiatry* 163 (2006): 28–40.

[142] U.S. Food and Drug Administration. "Guidance for industry and FDA staff—Class II special controls guidance document: Repetitive transcranial magnetic stimulation (rTMS) systems." July 26, 2011, updated June 5, 2015.

[143] Liston C, et al. "Default mode network mechanisms of transcranial magnetic stimulation in depression." *Biological Psychiatry* 76, no. 7 (2014): 517–26.

[144] Dierckx B, Heijen WT, et al. "Efficacy of electroconvulsive therapy in bipolar versus unipolar major depression: A meta-analysis." *Bipolar Disorders* 14, no. 2 (March 2012): 146–50.

[145] Pies R. "Are antidepressants effective in the acute and long-term treatment of depression? *Sic et non.*" *Innovations in Clinical Neuroscience* 9, no. 5–6 (May–June 2012): 31–40.

[146] McDonald W, Weiner R, and McCall WV. "The FDA and ECT." *Journal of ECT* 32, no. 2 (June 2016): 75–77. doi: 10.1097/YCT.0000000000000326.

[147] Perrin JS, et al. "Electroconvulsive therapy reduces frontal cortical connectivity in severe depression disorder." *Proceedings of the National Academy of Sciences USA* 109 (2012): 5464–68.

[148] Abbott CC, et al. "Hippocampal structural and functional changes associated with electroconvulsive therapy response." *Translational Psychiatry* 4, no. 11 (November 2014): 4e 483. doi: 10.1038/tp.2014.124.

[149] Breggin P. "Disturbing news for patients and shock doctors alike." The Huffington Post. May 25, 2011.

[150] Sadowsky J. "Electroconvulsive therapy: A history of controversy, but also of help." *Scientific American.* January 13, 2017.

[151] Nelson JC, Spyker DA. "Morbidity and mortality associated with medications used in the treatment of depression: An analysis of cases reported to U.S. poison control centers, 2000–2014." *American Journal of Psychiatry* 174 (2017): 438–50. doi: 10.1176/appi.ajp.2016.16050523.

[152] Breggin P. *Toxic Psychiatry: Why Therapy, Empathy and Love Must Replace the Drugs, Electroshock, and Biochemical Theories of the "New Psychiatry."* New York: St. Martin's Press, 1991.

[153] Szasz, T. *The Myth of Mental Illness.* New York: Harper Perennial, 2010.

[154] Ma H, Marti-Gutierrez N, Park S-W, et al. "Correction of a pathogenic gene mutation in human embryos." *Nature.* August 2, 2017. doi:10.1038/nature23305.

[155] Jeste DV, et al. "Association between older age and more successful aging: Critical role of resilience and depression." *American Journal of Psychiatry* 170, no. 2 (2013): 188–96. doi: 10.1176/appi.ajp2012.1200000.

Index

About the Author

*A*uthor, public speaker, professor, and mental healthcare advo-
cate **Bick Wanck, MD**, personifies the term *passionate*. He is the
recipient of multiple awards, including Best Doctors of America Best Doctors Award, Psychiatry, Capital District (Albany, NY) for numerous years.

A board-certified psychiatrist, he is the founder of Bick Wanck, MD &
Associates, a successful and highly regarded private mental health group
practice with twenty-five clinicians in two clinics. As one of the founders of
the American Academy of Addiction Psychiatry, he helped to develop the
nationally certified subspecialty of addiction psychiatry. He is an assistant
professor of clinical psychiatry at Albany Medical School, and he also held
that position at both Rutgers University and the University of Medicine
and Dentistry of New Jersey. He's taught hundreds of medical students and
residents, has lectured in Grand Rounds seminars at many medical schools,
and was featured in a series of educational films showing the art of diag-
nostic interviewing for medical students, nurses, and psychiatry residents.

Bick Wanck's speaking career started at age fifteen with a series of talks
about SCUBA diving for civic groups, schools, and professional organizations. During medical school, he helped to develop and run a speakers'
bureau with his mentor, John E. Fryer, MD, who declared, in 1972, that
homosexuality is not an illness. Dr. Fryer encouraged him to work directly
with the speakers, who included Margaret Mead, Gloria Steinem, Alex
Comfort (*The Joy of Sex*), and Buckminster Fuller, among others.

No stranger to celebrity, Bick had the pleasure of speaking alongside Jay Leno at an international humor conference, and he toured for several years with the leading writers and speakers for the codependency self-help movement, speaking alongside Jan Woititz (*Adult Children of Alcoholics* and others), John Bradshaw (*Healing the Shame That Binds You* and a PBS series of the same title), Patrick Carnes (*Out of the Shadows,* about sex addiction; *Don't Call It Love*; and others), Sharon Wegscheider-Cruse and her husband, Joe Cruse (the Betty Ford Center), and others.

Before starting his own practice, he ran the addiction treatment programs in a private psychiatric hospital in New Jersey. There he treated movie stars, rock stars, porn stars, and politicians.

Following that experience, he created Bick Wanck, MD & Associates. There he developed the concept of a Three-Layered Healing Plan, which has successfully helped thousands of people over the course of thirty years.

His academic publications include a lead article in the *American Journal of Psychiatry,* a piece in *JAMA* (*Journal of the American Medical Association*), and a chapter in a psychiatry textbook, along with other published writings.

On a personal note, Bick writes, "What qualifies me most to write this book is my personal journey of recovery, wellness, and growth. After years of violent and otherwise challenging circumstances growing up in a poor rural area and then living in a crime-ridden poor inner-city neighborhood, I learned the values of perseverance, persistence, and determination. By necessity, I sought healing for myself. My mission became helping others to do the same. I know what it's like to suffer, and I know what it's like to get well and flourish. I learned about the essential nature and process of healing and promoting healing the hard way. My calling and passion are to help others find their own way to wellness."

Bick is an avid traveler, scuba diver, and surfer who makes his home with his wife on a lake in upstate New York. His two grown daughters give him good reason to travel. One lives on Maui, where she helps to run Lumeria Maui, a spiritual retreat center. The other lives in Connecticut (and surfs in Rhode Island) and is an educator and social activist.